Mel Bay's

# BLUES

## LEAD GUITAR METHOD

D1919583

**by Steve Griffin**

### CD CONTENTS



MEL BAY®




*Visit us on the Web at http://www.melbay.com — E-mail us at email@melbay.com*

1 2 3 4 5 6 7 8 9 0

Mel Bay's

# BLUES

LEAD GUITAR METHOD

by Steve Griffin

## INDEX

Mel Bay's

# BLUES

LEAD GUITAR METHOD

by Steve Griffin

# FOREWORD

Playing lead Blues-Rock guitar depends mainly on two things (1) what you can hear in your mind and (2) getting your fingers to the proper sounds on your instrument. This book was written with emphasis on the second idea. Hundreds of young guitar players have struggled hour after hour to find the sounds they want to hear, with no help except their "ear" and listening to records, etc. Some books have been published that present bits and pieces of the scales and patterns presented here, but stop short of a complete understandable and usable system. There are Four Blues-Rock finger patterns used in this book utilizing all six strings of the guitar with each pattern. These four patterns connect with each other enabling the lead player to use the entire fingerboard and range of the guitar to express his musical ideas. Charts are used to show you how to place these four patterns at the proper place on the neck for improvising in any key. Great Rock solos can be played in any one of these four patterns or in any combination of the patterns from one to four. You must memorize the finger patterns completely and get your fingers so familiar with each one that you can play them rapidly without even thinking about it before your musical "ear" can take over and complete the process of "improvising." Once you have accomplished this, you will realize that almost all the Rock-lead sounds you have heard are based on the positions you have learned. If you don't read music, it doesn't matter as each step in this book is shown in tablature (a number system which is fully explained). The basic instruction is here - now it is up to you to ROCK AND ROLL.

THE AUTHOR:

Steve Griffin - Performing musician and teacher for the past 15 years. Attended The University of North Carolina, and presently co-owner of the Neil Griffin Studios of Music, located in Charlotte, N.C., where this method has been studio tested and proven with students of all ages.

# READING TABLATURE

Tablature is simply a drawing of the 6 strings of the guitar with numbers showing you to-either pick a string open or in which fret to press a string down to produce the note called for in the music.

The tablature will appear throughout this book directly under each note of music showing which string and in which fret every note is found on the guitar.

Shown below are examples of tablature with an explanation of each item.

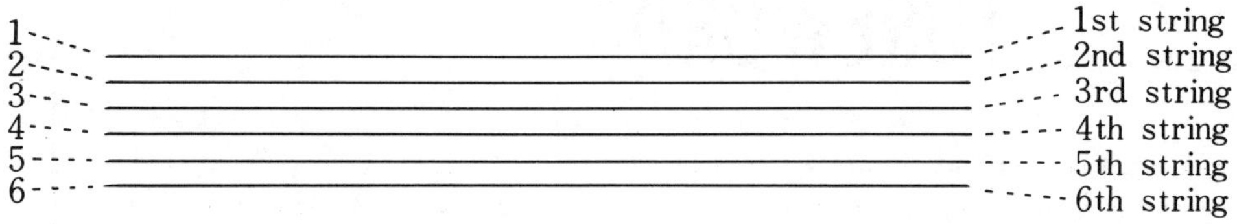


There are six lines in the tablature, one for each string on the guitar as shown above.

The numbers placed on the tablature lines show in which fret to press down the left hand fingers.

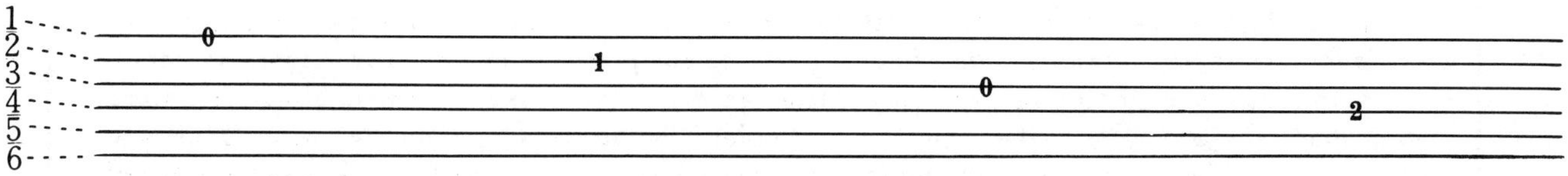


1st string
Open

2nd string
1st fret

3rd string
Open

4th string
2nd fret

When two or more notes are played at the same time, the numbers are above one another as shown below.

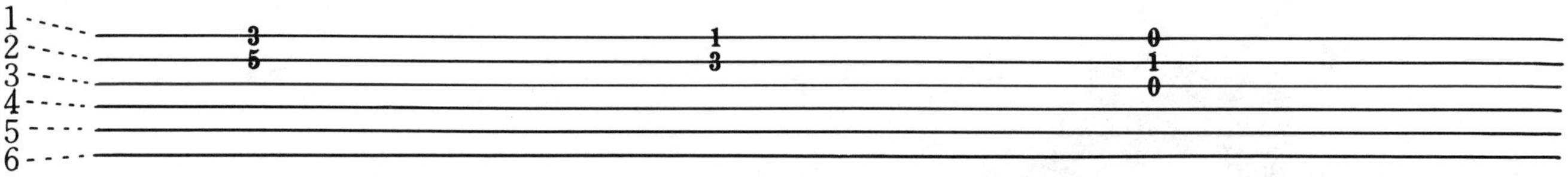


1st string-3rd fret
2nd string-5th fret

1st string-1st fret
2nd string-3rd fret

1st string-open
2nd string-1st fret
3rd string-open

# COUNTING TIME IN TABLATURE

Counting time in tablature will be exactly the same as in regular musical notation, using a time signature at the beginning, with measures separated by bar lines, and with stems being used for the different time values.

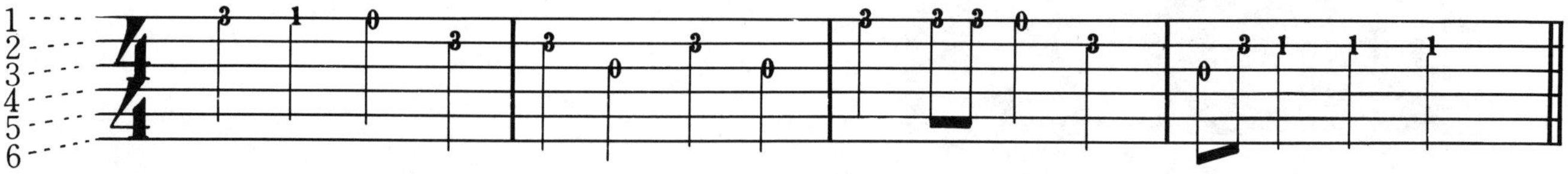


Count: 1 2 3 4 1 2 3 4 1 2 & 3 4 1 & 2 3 4

The only difference in tablature counting will be that if a note is to be held longer than one count, it will be shown as follows:

The first count will have the regular quarter note stem and will be connected to one additional quarter note stem for each additional count the note is to be held.

NOTE: Although you may know how to read standard notation, it will be helpful to refer to the tablature to make sure notes are played in the best playing position.

# GUITAR FINGERBOARD

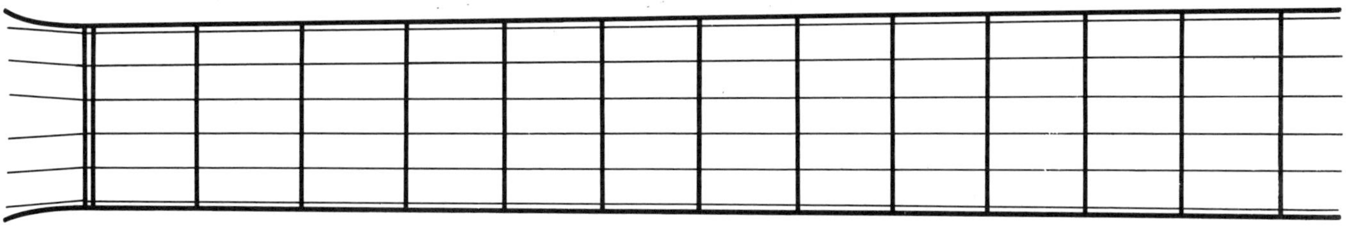

# INTRODUCING BLUES SCALE I IN NOTES AND TABLATURE

THE FOLLOWING DIAGRAM SHOWS THE CORRECT FINGERING FOR THIS BLUES SCALE AND HOW IT APPEARS ON THE FINGERBOARD FOR THE KEY OF G MAJOR:

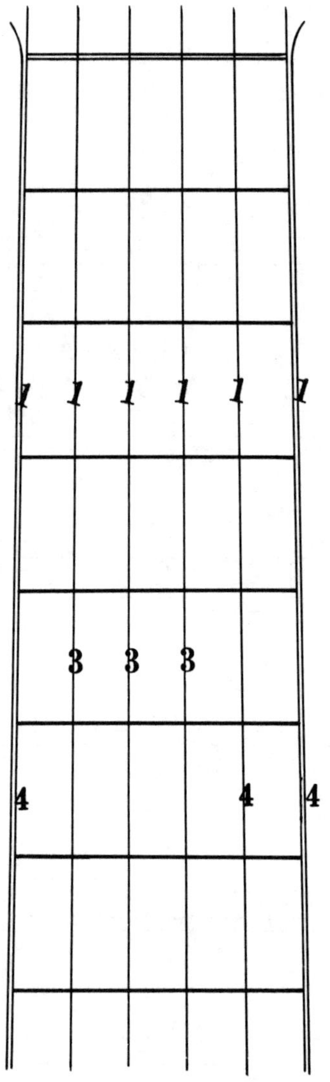


This Blues Scale is in the key of G Major, 1st finger is playing G note - 1st string, 3rd fret.

Practice this Blues Scale Pattern forwards and backwards (low to high, and high to low).

Using the correct fingering, play the following sequence of notes. Start on number one, then play numbers two, three, four, and so on until you reach number twelve.

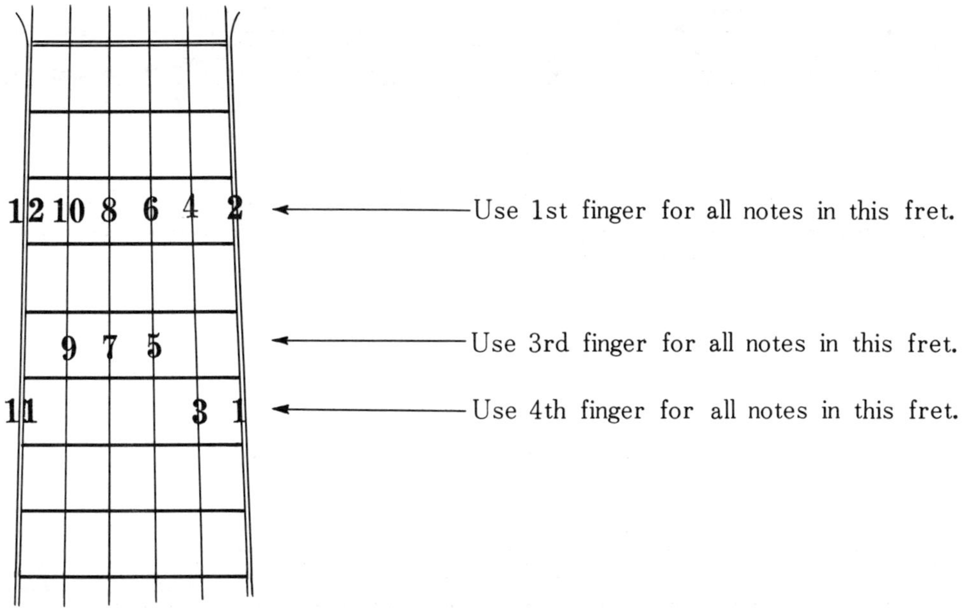


Playing these twelve notes should give you some feeling of direction in starting your fingers to move from note to note within this blues scale.

# ADDITIONAL SEQUENCES TO TRY

As you look at the above diagram, play the notes in the following order:

| | | | | | | | | | | | | | | | | | | |
|---|---|---|---|---|---|---|---|---|---|---|---|---|---|---|---|---|---|---|
| -- 12 | 11 | 10 | 9 | 8 | 7 | 6 | 5 | 4 | 3 | 2 | 1 | | | | | | | |
| -- 5 | 6 | 5 | 4 | 5 | 6 | 7 | 8 | 10 | 9 | 8 | 7 | 6 | 7 | 5 | 7 | | | |
| -- 1 | 2 | 1 | 2 | 3 | 2 | 3 | 4 | 5 | 4 | 5 | 6 | 7 | | | | | | |
| -- 1 | 1 | 1 | 2 | 2 | 2 | 3 | 3 | 3 | 4 | 4 | 4 | 5 | 5 | 5 | 6 | 6 | 6 | 7 |
| -- 12 | 12 | 7 | 7 | 8 | 8 | 9 | 9 | 12 | 12 | 7 | 7 | 8 | 8 | 9 | 9 | 12 | | |

Now that you know how this scale sounds and the correct fingering, you are ready for your first lead guitar solo. Be sure you understand how to read tablature, page 2.

As you play the solo on the following page, notice that all notes are taken from Blues Scale I, page 4. If you have the scale memorized and have a clear mental picture of how the scale "looks" when played on the fingerboard, then with the help of the tablature your fingers should fall into place.

# LEAD SOLO USING BLUES SCALE I

# ANOTHER SOLO USING ONLY NOTES FROM BLUES SCALE I

# RHYTHM GUITAR CHORDS

For the Rhythm Guitar, the most commonly used twelve measure blues accompaniment is illustrated below. There are many accompaniment variations that the Blues Scale will work with, but for now learn this one.

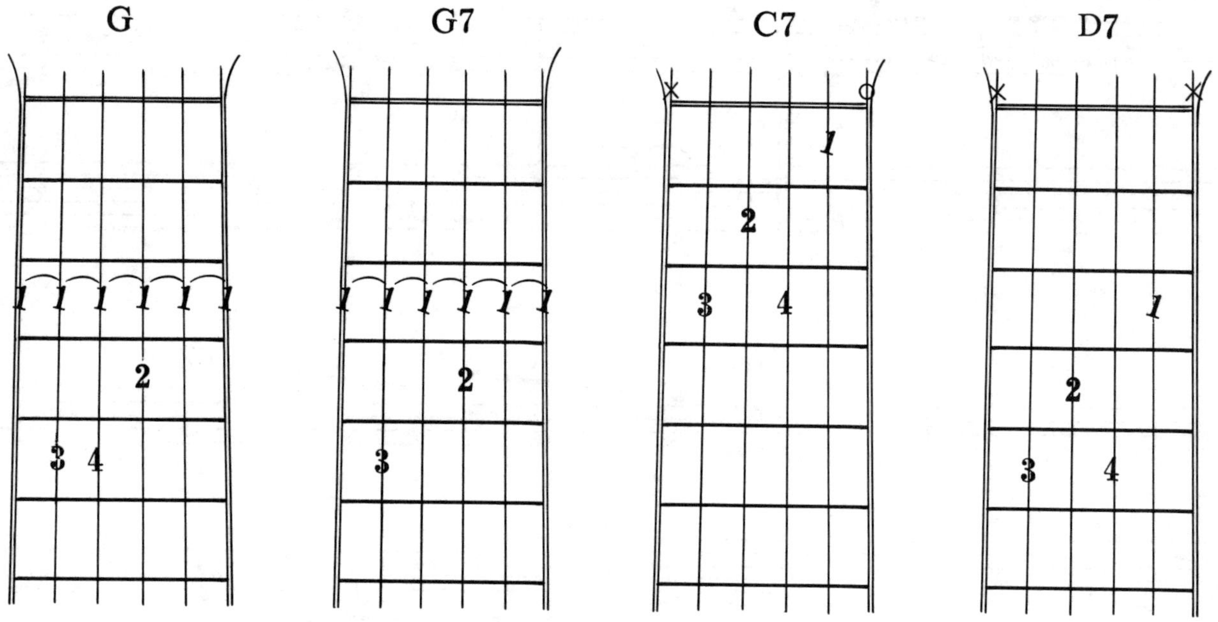


# 12 BAR BLUES ACCOMPANIMENT IN THE KEY OF G

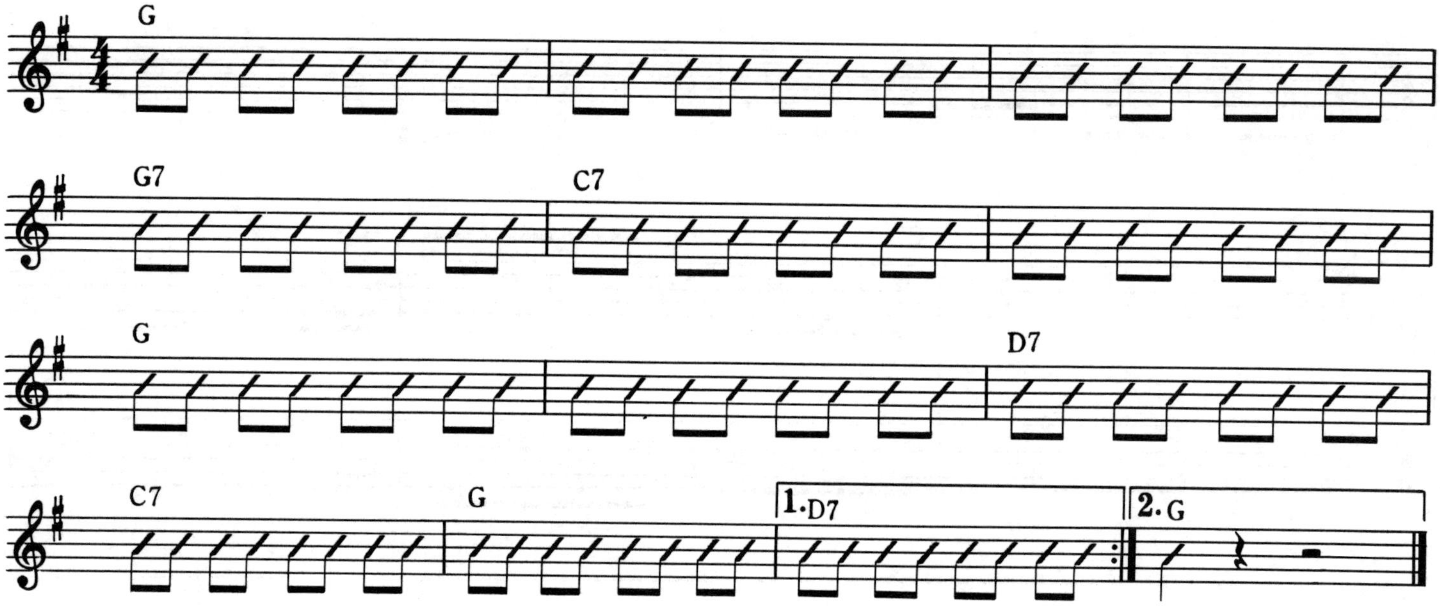


Learning this progression will be very helpful when you begin to construct your own blues lead choruses. Working on the chords should be the first thing you do when learning a song-this is the foundation. In the example above, play all eighth note chord symbols with a down pick and count as:

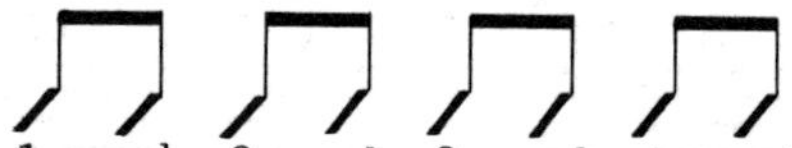

1 and 2 and 3 and 4 and

# TECHNIQUES

As you keep the Blues Scale in mind, look at some of the following Blues and Rock Techniques. These techniques give each lead improvising chorus a real flavor of down home blues.

BENDING To bend or choke a note, press firmly on the string and push the string towards the bass or large strings on the guitar. As the string stretches, the pitch of the note raises slightly (usually $\frac{1}{2}$ - $1\frac{1}{2}$ steps). A bend is indicated by the symbol: **Bend**

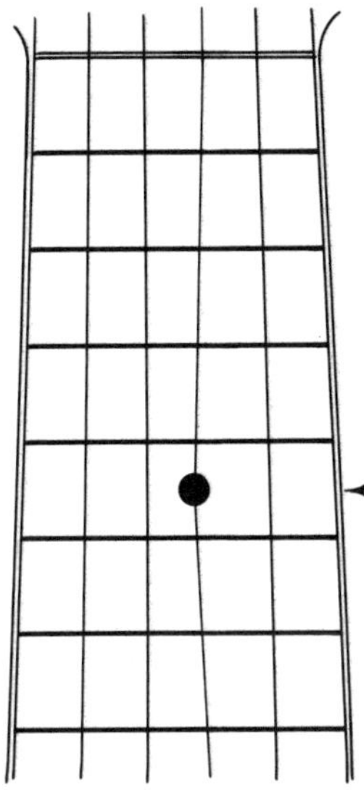

In this example, the Bend occurs on the 3rd string, 5th fret.

As you play over the Blues Scale, try bending the notes indicated in the following diagrams. The bending note will be marked with an X.

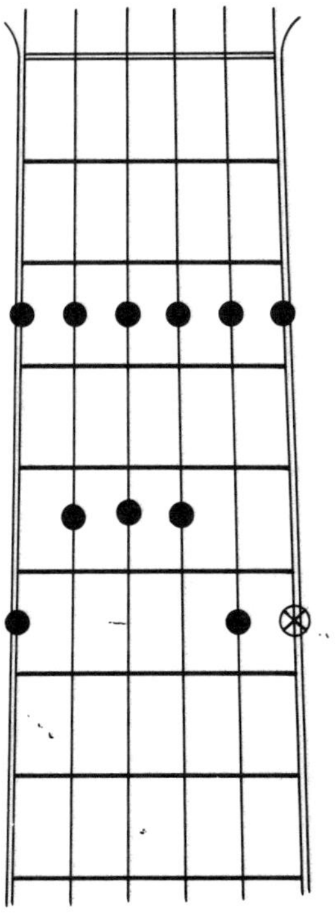

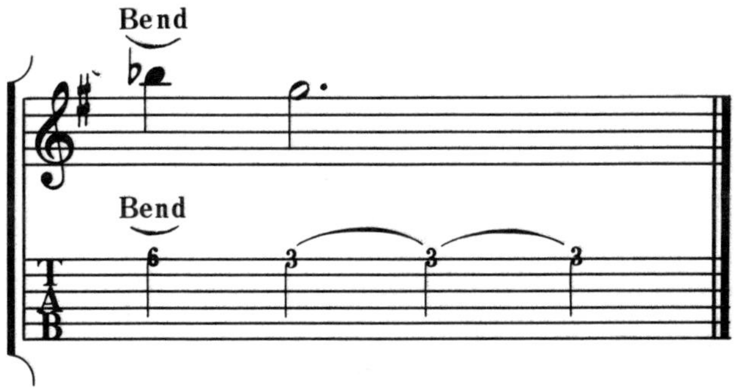

# BENDING EXERCISES CONTINUED

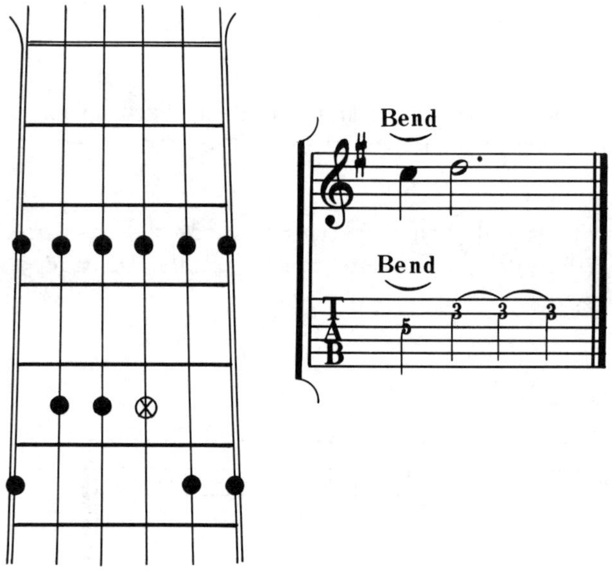


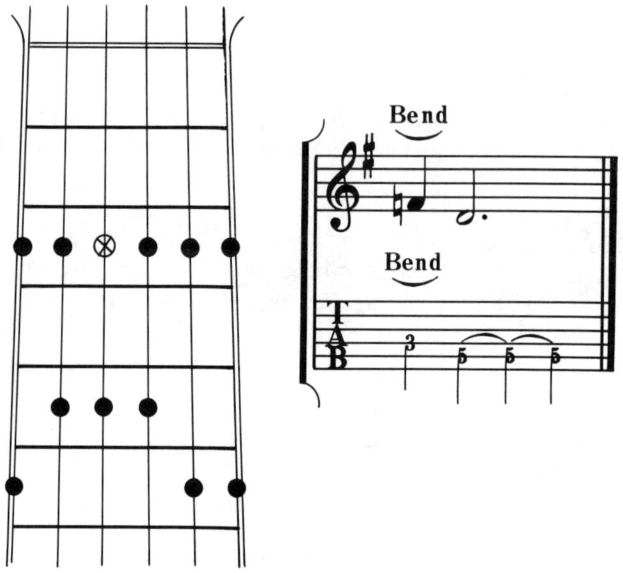


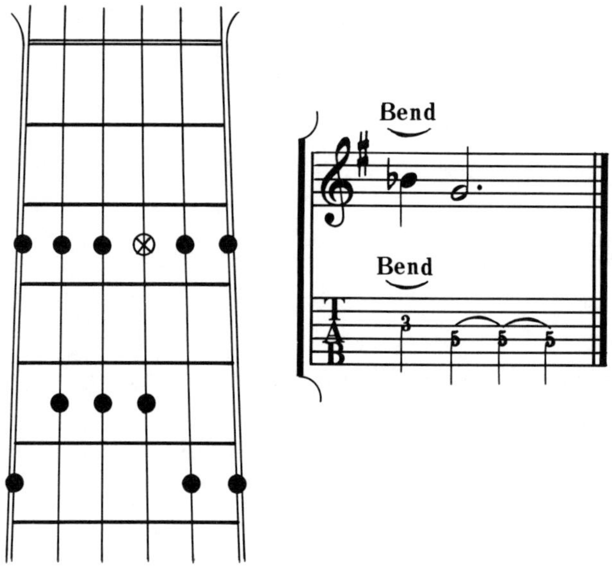


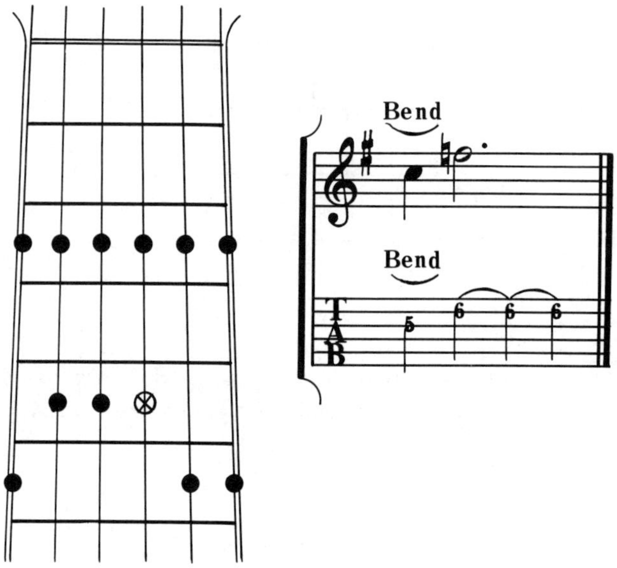


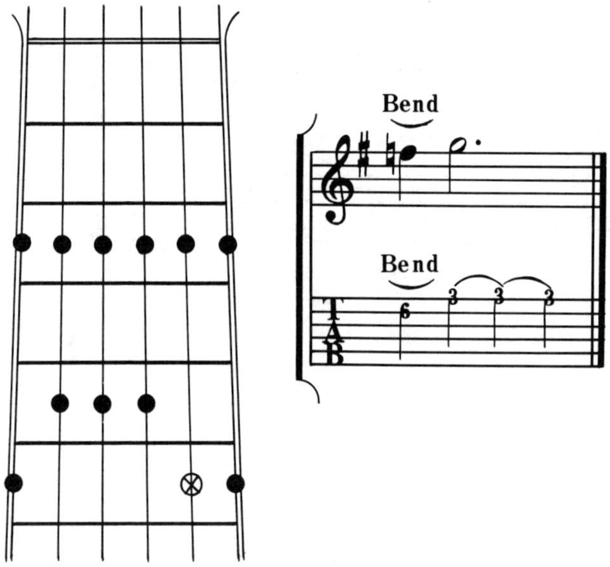


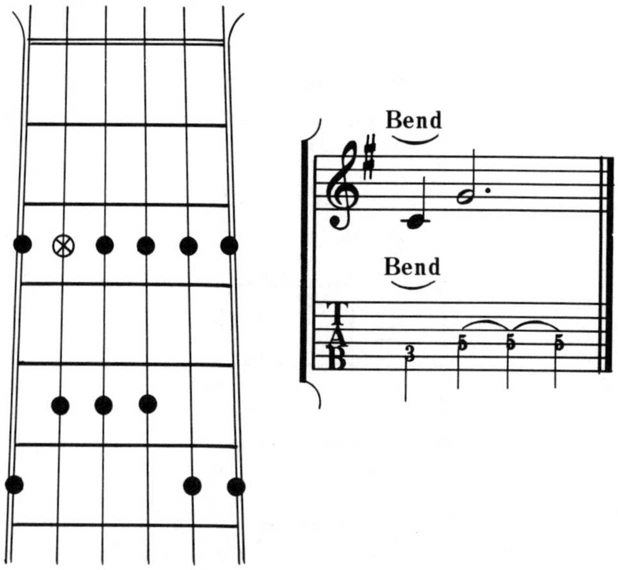

# BENDING SOLO

The following solo is an example of tasteful bending.
Notice that this technique is not over-used.

**SLIDE** The slide technique is a simple effect that can be used with any note in the Blues Scale. When sliding up to a note, begin the slide from a lower fret and slide upward until the desired note is reached. This is usually a sliding distance of one to four frets. As the slide occurs, do not pick each note; only the first note is picked – then slide. Slide the same finger that will be used on the final note. A slide is indicated by the symbol: /

In the following example, place the 3rd finger on the 3rd string at the 3rd fret. Holding the note firmly, pick the note and slide the 3rd finger up to the 5th fret.

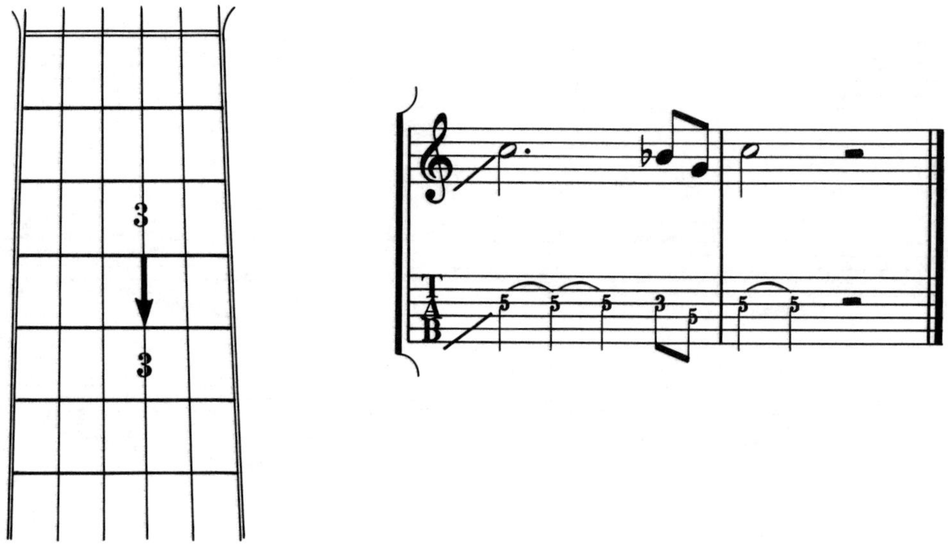

Try sliding other notes within the Blues Scale. You can slide into any note in the scale. For example:

# SLIDE SOLO

An Example Solo of the Slide Technique.

**VIBRATO** Vibrato is a pulsating effect that is very helpful when sustaining a note. It is achieved by picking a note once, then moving the finger back and forth rapidly within the fret. As the finger moves back and forth on the string, the pitch raises and lowers. This technique gives the note a colorful, wavy sound. The symbol for Vibrato is: VIB.

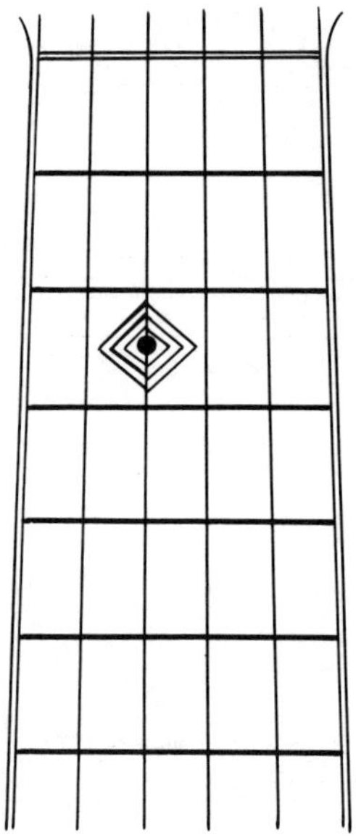

In this example, the Vibrato technique is played on the 4th string, 3rd fret.

Move the finger back and forth in the fret from side to side very rapidly keeping pressure on the string, slightly varying the musical pitch.

As you play over the Blues Scale, try using vibrato on some of the notes indicated in the following diagrams. Notes using vibrato will be marked by: 

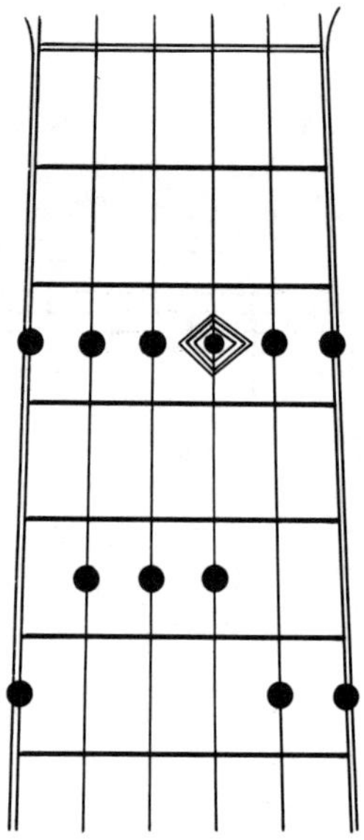

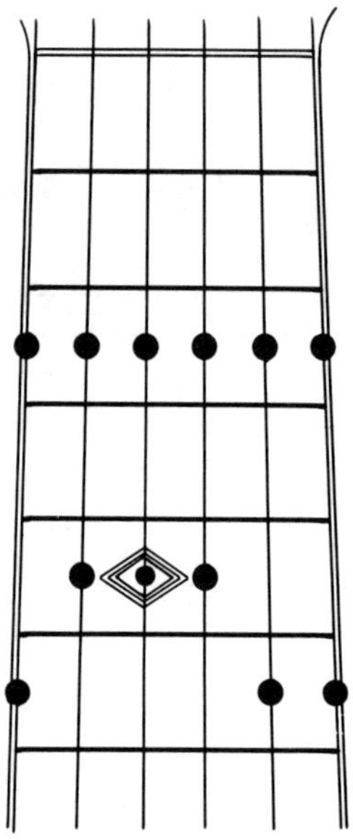

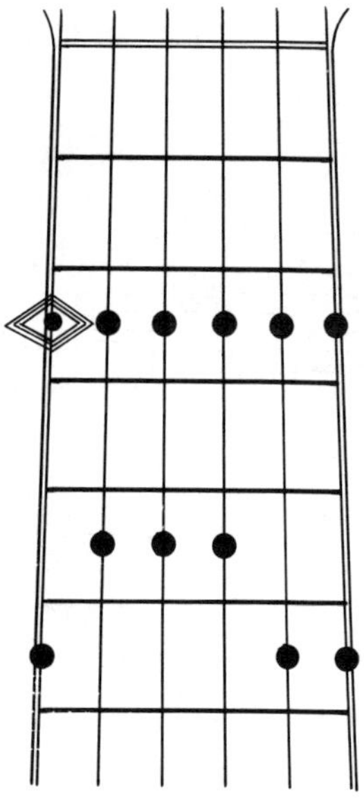

# SOLO USING VIBRATO

This solo is an example of the vibrato technique; however, notice the bending and sliding techniques are also used. In combining techniques, you can make solos much more interesting and professional.

**DOUBLE NOTES** Double notes are often used to give "body" and strength to lead guitar solos. This is simply a technique of playing two notes at one time. Play the double notes in the following example. Be sure not to pick the notes individually, but together as if you were playing a chord.

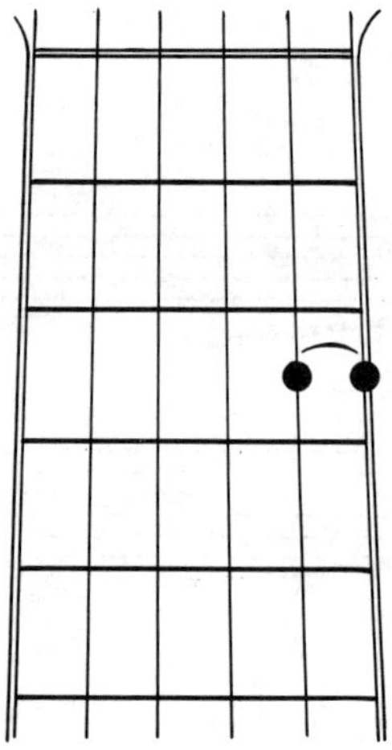

In this example, the double notes are G, 1st string – 3rd fret and D, 2nd string – 3rd fret.

In musical notation and tablature, double notes are written above one another as shown below.

# DOUBLE NOTE COMBINATIONS TAKEN FROM BLUES SCALE I

Try some of the following combinations of double notes.
Keep in mind that all notes in the examples are taken from Blues Scale I. (p. 4)

**Ex. 1**

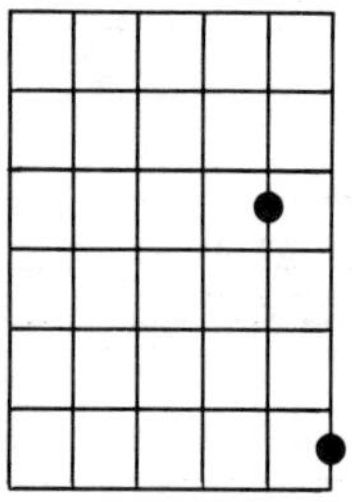

**Ex. 2**

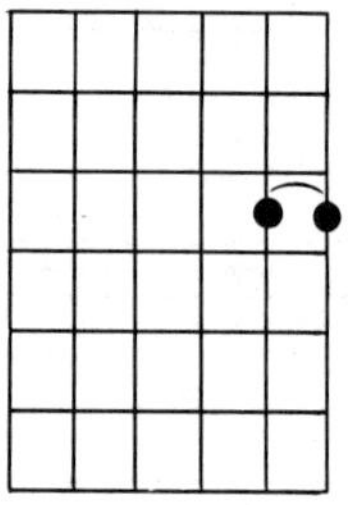

**Ex. 3**

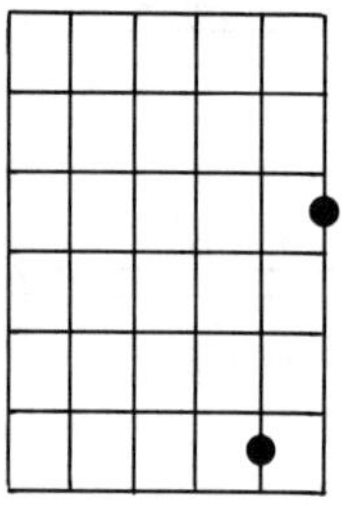

**Ex. 4**

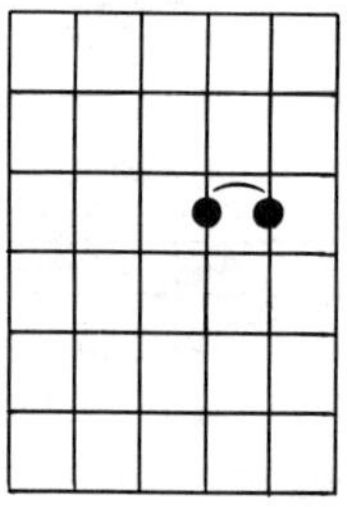

**Ex. 5**

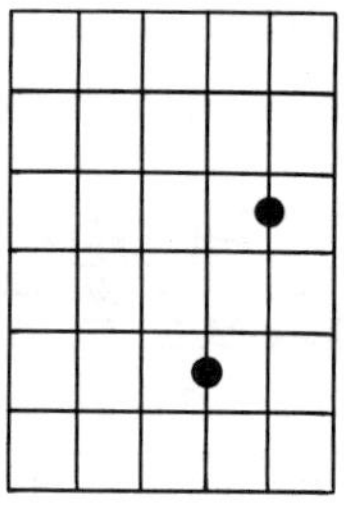

**Ex. 6**

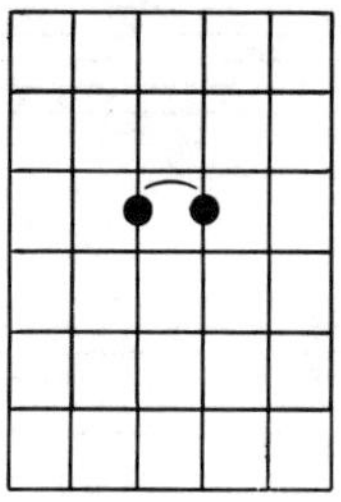

**Ex. 7**

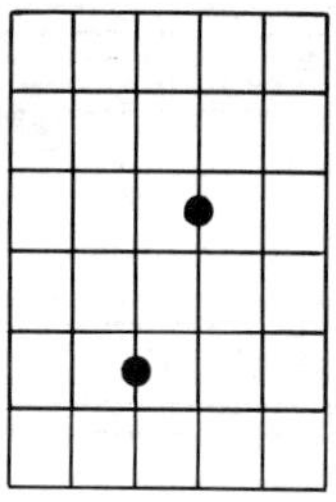

**Ex. 8**

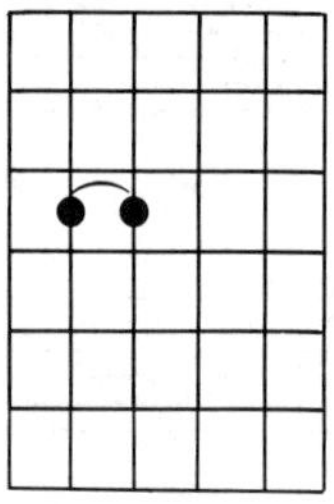

**Ex. 9**

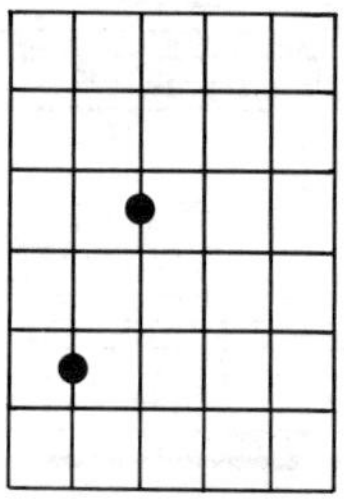

**Ex. 10**

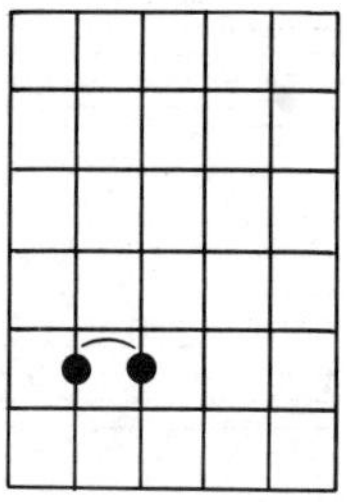

**Ex. 11**

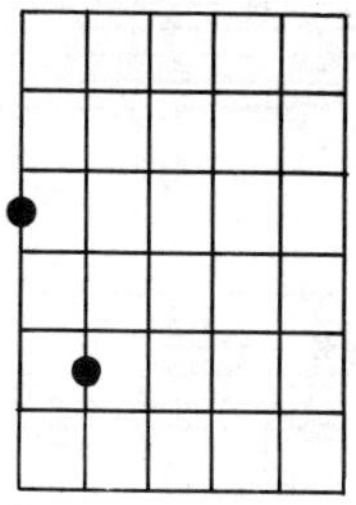

# SOLO USING THE DOUBLE NOTE TECHNIQUE

**For Further Study See Mel Bay's Deluxe Anthology Of Rock Guitar**

# CAN YOU CONSTRUCT A BLUES--ROCK SOLO?

Have the RHYTHM GUITAR play the progression shown below:

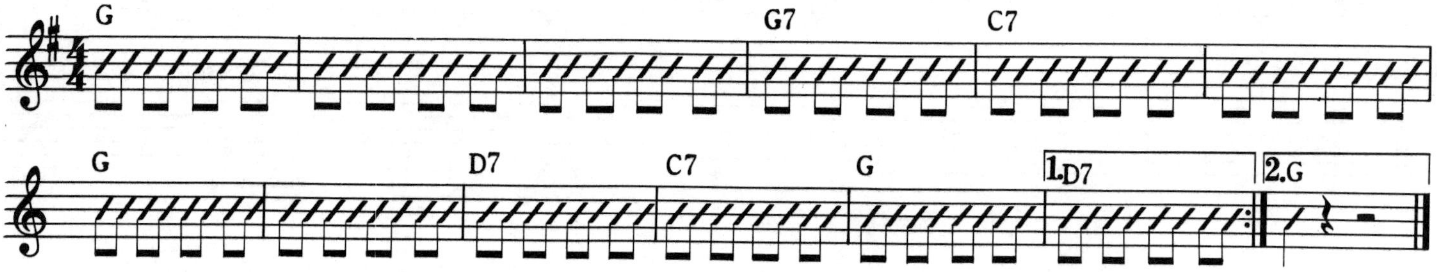


As the LEAD GUITAR, you will play notes from Blues Scale I. The most interesting thing to learn about this scale is the fact that any note in the scale will work with any chord in the twelve-bar progression above. Start with any note you want to within the scale and play with feeling using different rhythms. As you try to make your solo melodic, occasionally use one of the techniques of bending, sliding, vibrato, or double notes.

If it is very difficult at this point to make up a blues solo, then go back and review, even memorize, some of the solos that have been written as examples. Carefully study how the solos begin and how the techniques are used.

# A WORD ABOUT RHYTHM

This book is written with the assumption that you already know time values of notes and rests.
If you need to learn rhythm and counting, you may refer to MODERN GUITAR METHOD by Mel Bay.

In constructing an interesting solo, you must be completely knowledgeable and at ease with rhythm.

The following is a basic chart of time values of notes and rests:

| | | | |
|---|---|---|---|
| **WHOLE NOTE** | **WHOLE REST** | | **4 COUNTS** |
| **DOTTED HALF NOTE** | **DOTTED HALF REST** | | **3 COUNTS** |
| **HALF NOTE** | **HALF REST** | | **2 COUNTS** |
| **QUARTER NOTE** | **QUARTER REST** | | **1 COUNT** |
| **EIGHTH NOTE** | **EIGHTH REST** | | **1/2 COUNT** |
| **SIXTEENTH NOTE** | **SIXTEENTH REST** | | **1/4 COUNT** |

NOTE : Two Eighth notes may be written ♪ ♪ or ♫

Two Sixteenth notes may be written ♬ ♬ or ♬

As the lead guitar, you must know how to combine these time values and other advanced rhythmic ideas in interesting and clever ways. As an example, rhythmically your notes might be combined as follows:

**NOW THAT YOU KNOW SOME FUNDAMENTAL ROCK TECHNIQUES AND HAVE ATTEMPTED TO MAKE UP AN ORIGINAL SOLO, YOU NEED TO KNOW HOW TO PLAY UP AND DOWN THE GUITAR FINGERBOARD.**

**THE NEXT SECTION DEALS WITH THIS CONCEPT OF PLAYING UP AND DOWN THE GUITAR NECK—IN EVERY KEY.**

# BLUES SCALE PATTERNS I-II-III-IV

Memorize the following four blues scale patterns and be sure you understand pattern positioning (p. 21) before you proceed. Each scale pattern should be practiced forwards and backwards (low to high, and high to low). You should already know Scale I.

I

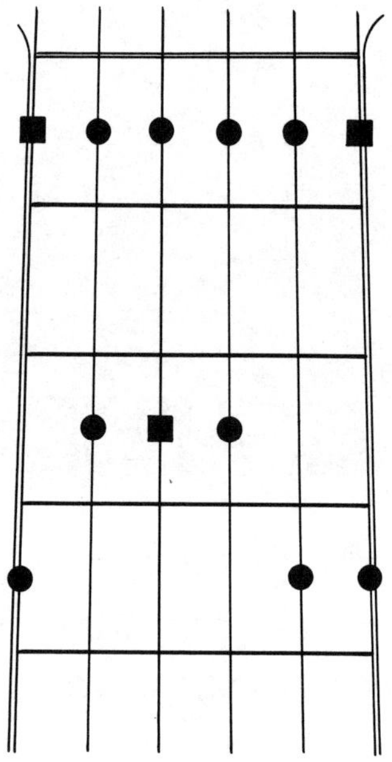

II

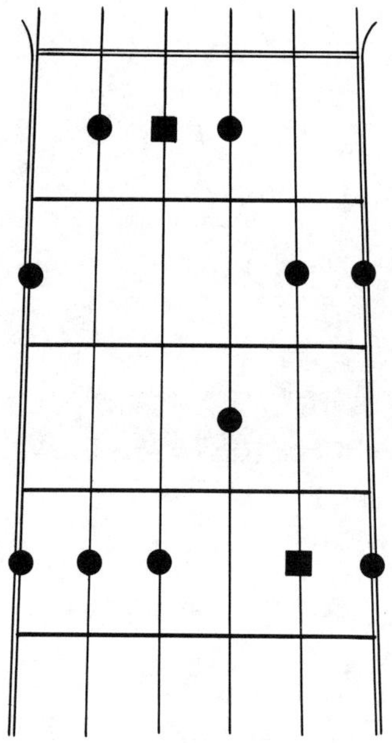

III

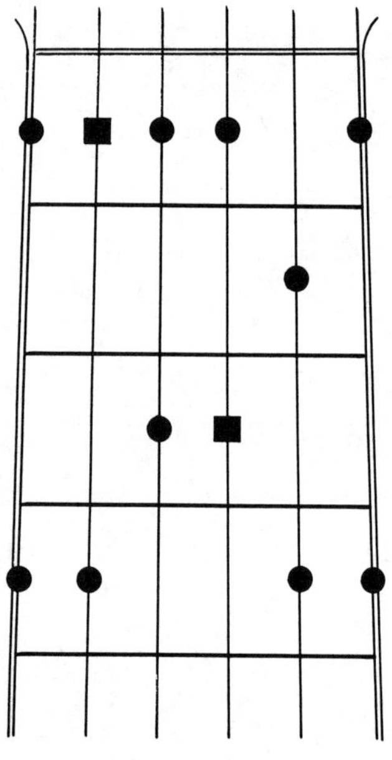

IV

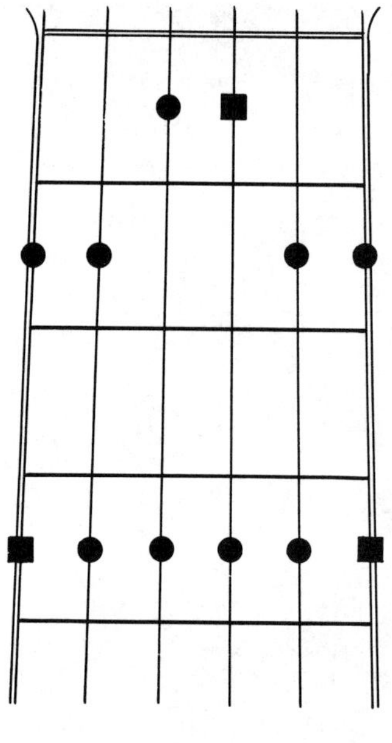

NOTE: Key tones are indicated by the symbol. ■ Almost all lead solos end on these notes.

# PATTERN POSITIONING

Positioning on the guitar is determined by the PLACEMENT OF THE FIRST FINGER. Each position covers four adjacent frets and when moving up the neck never uses open strings.

## IN THE FIRST POSITION

The first finger is in the first fret.
The second finger is in the second fret.
The third finger is in the third fret.
The fourth finger is in the fourth fret.

## IN THE SECOND POSITION

The first finger is in the second fret.
The second finger is in the third fret.
The third finger is in the fourth fret.
The fourth finger is in the fifth fret.

The average cut-away guitar should play up to approximately the seventeenth position (first finger placed in the seventeenth fret).

Study the following examples of positioning as applied to the Blues Scale Patterns. Remember the first finger determines the position.

### PATTERN I AT POSITION 3

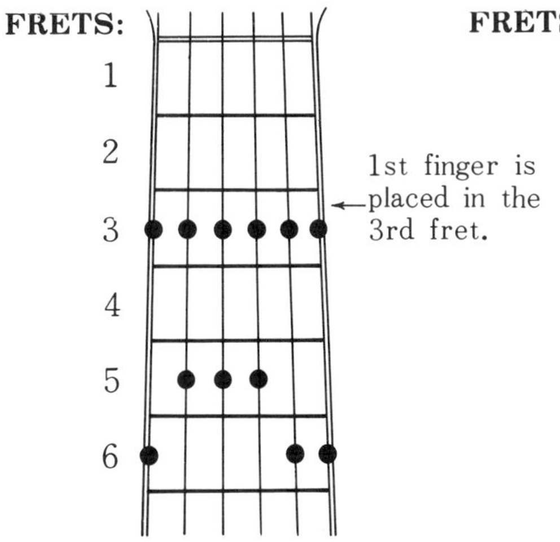


### PATTERN IV AT POSITION 5

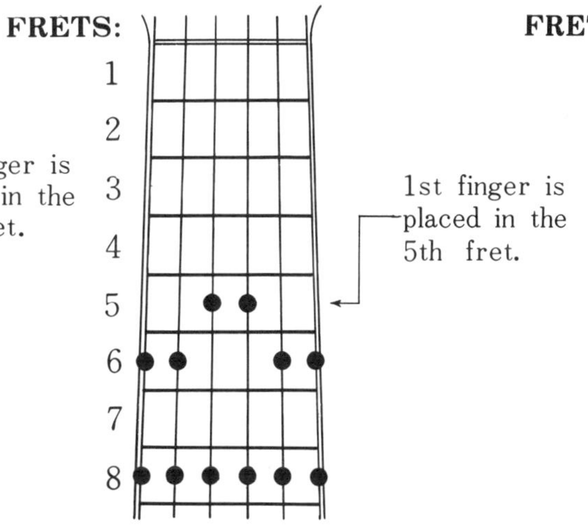


### OPEN-STRING PATTERN

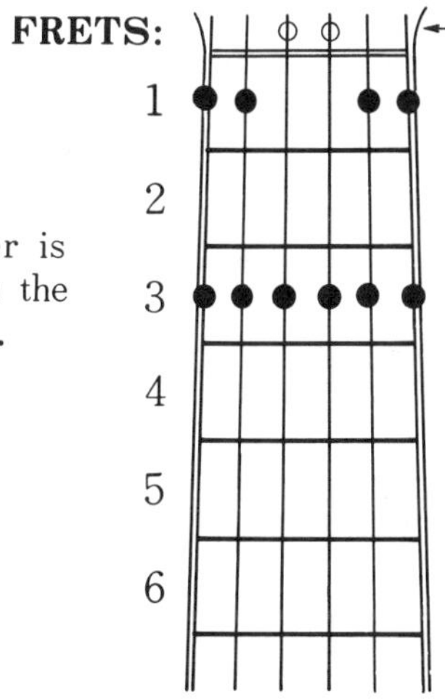


Occasionally it is necessary to use open strings to learn a key completely.

Naturally all open string patterns will be illustrated in the first position AT THE NUT so that the open strings can be utilized.

After you have memorized patterns I, II, III, and IV and thoroughly understand how to position them on the fingerboard, you are ready for a more practical application in KEY STUDY.

# KEY STUDY

As an example, let's study the key of F Major. The chart below shows where to position the four Blues Scale Patterns in order to play in the key of F.
(This positioning is the same for the key of F minor.)

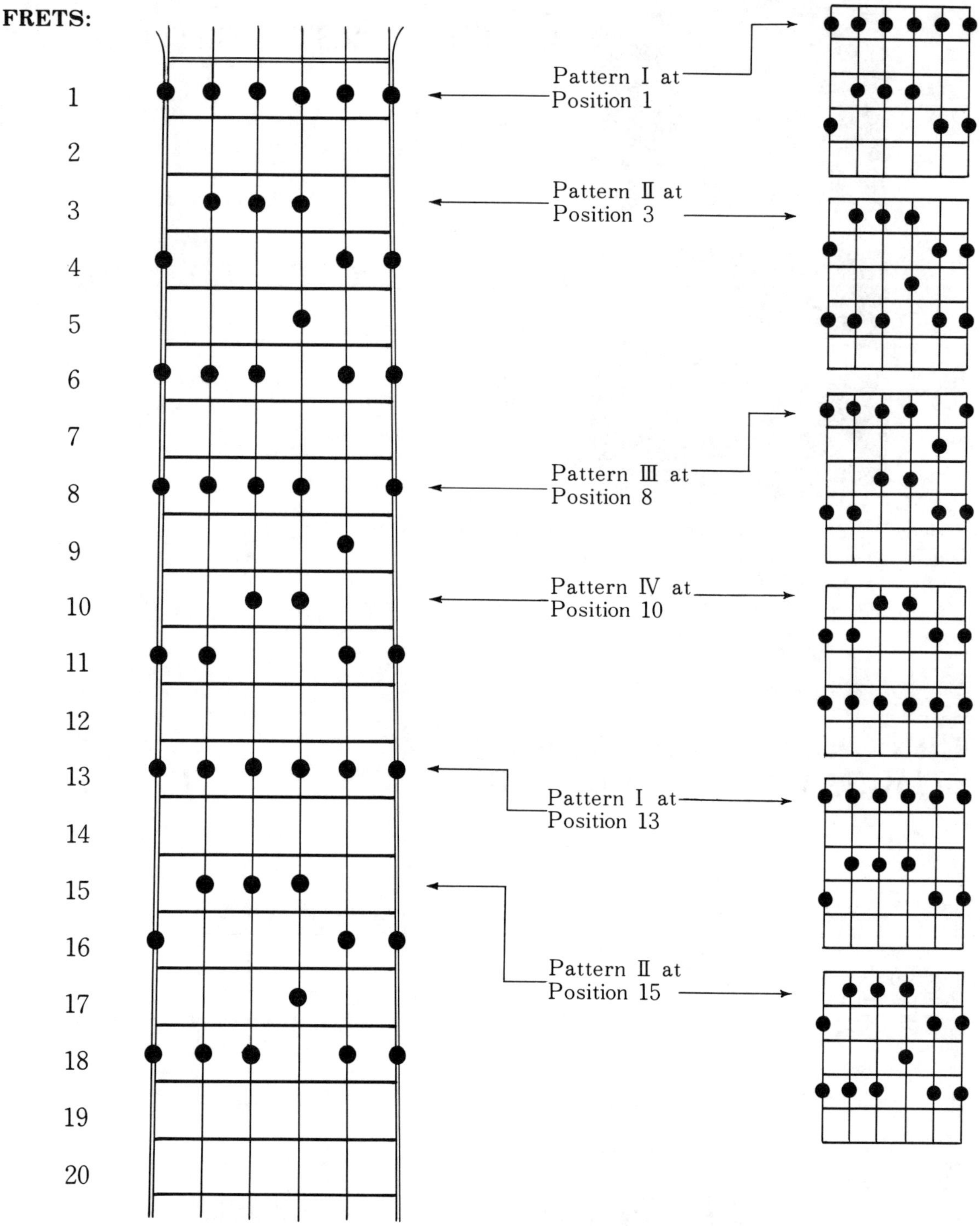


Try to play Patterns I, II, III, and IV up the neck as shown above without looking at this chart. All you have to do is keep in mind how to POSITION the patterns-that is FRETS 1, 3, 8, 10, 13, and 15.

# THE USE OF REFERENCE CHARTS

As you wish to study a key and learn notes to improvise with, you can consult the reference charts from pages **25** through **36**. These charts will give you the order in which to place the four scale patterns for EVERY KEY.

## PRACTICING VERTICALLY

Up to this point you have played Blues Scale I VERTICALLY (across the fingerboard from the first string to the sixth string and then back from the sixth string to the first string staying within a four fret area). All four basic patterns should first be learned in this manner.
Below is an illustration of vertical playing for the key of F.

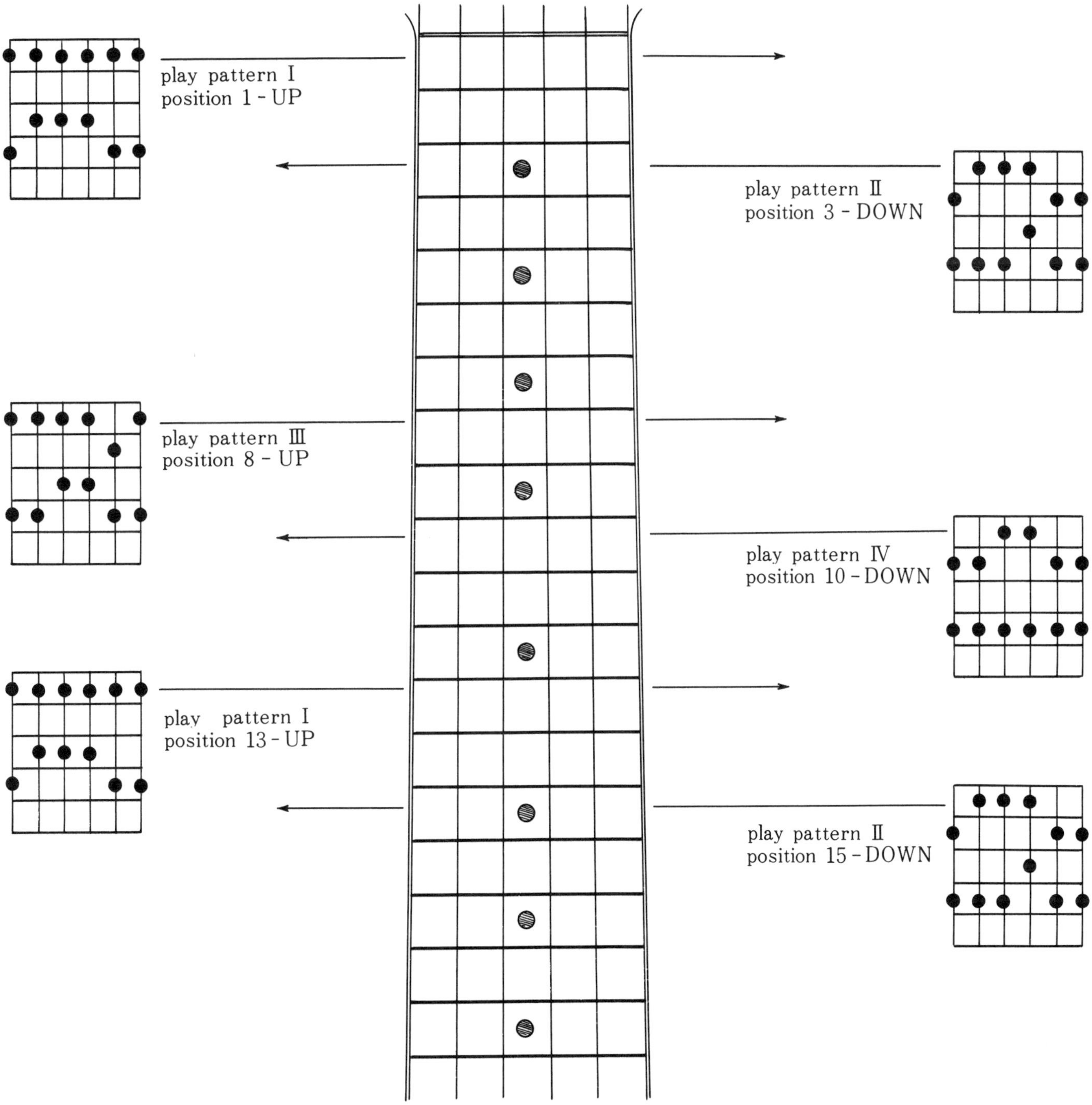

# PRACTICING HORIZONTALLY

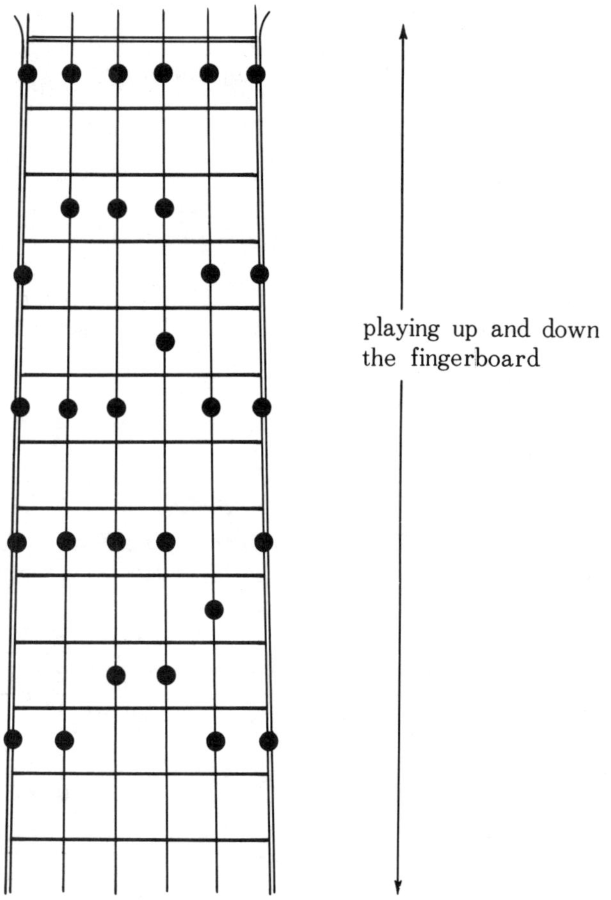


In horizontal practicing, the object is to play UP and DOWN the fingerboard using the full length key diagrams.
These diagrams are located on the reference charts for every key. Horizontal practicing is probably the most profitable way to practice. If you study long and hard enough in each key, soon the "pattern barrier" will disappear and you will begin to play notes not only vertically (across the strings), but horizontally (up and down the fingerboard) blending the four blues scale patterns into one complete scope of the guitar neck.

As an example of horizontal playing, try the following sequence of numbers:

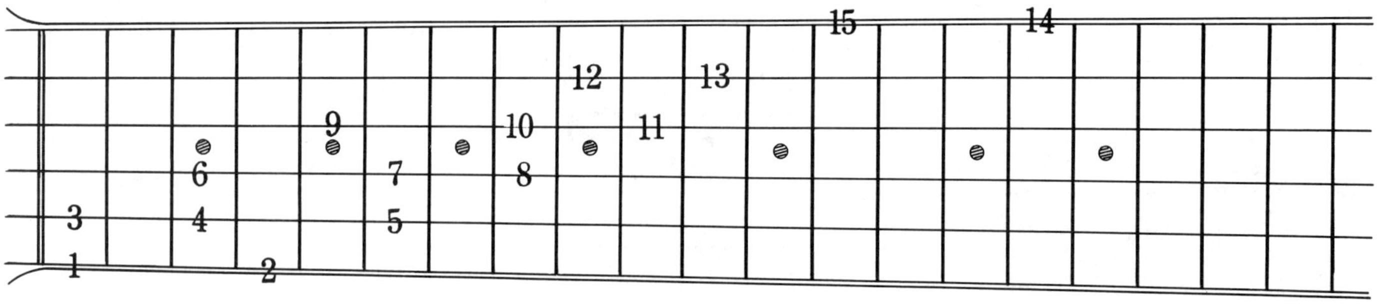


# KEEP IN MIND

As you practice from the reference charts, play VERTICALLY and HORIZONTALLY.
Play with feeling and try to construct exciting rhythmic ideas.
Don't forget to apply techniques of bending, sliding, vibrato, and double notes.

# REFERENCE CHARTS
# KEY OF F Major and F Minor

Key Signatures:

F
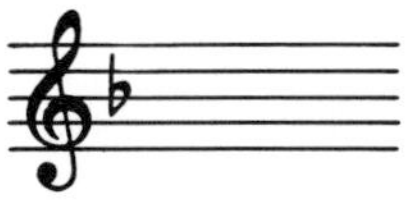

Fm

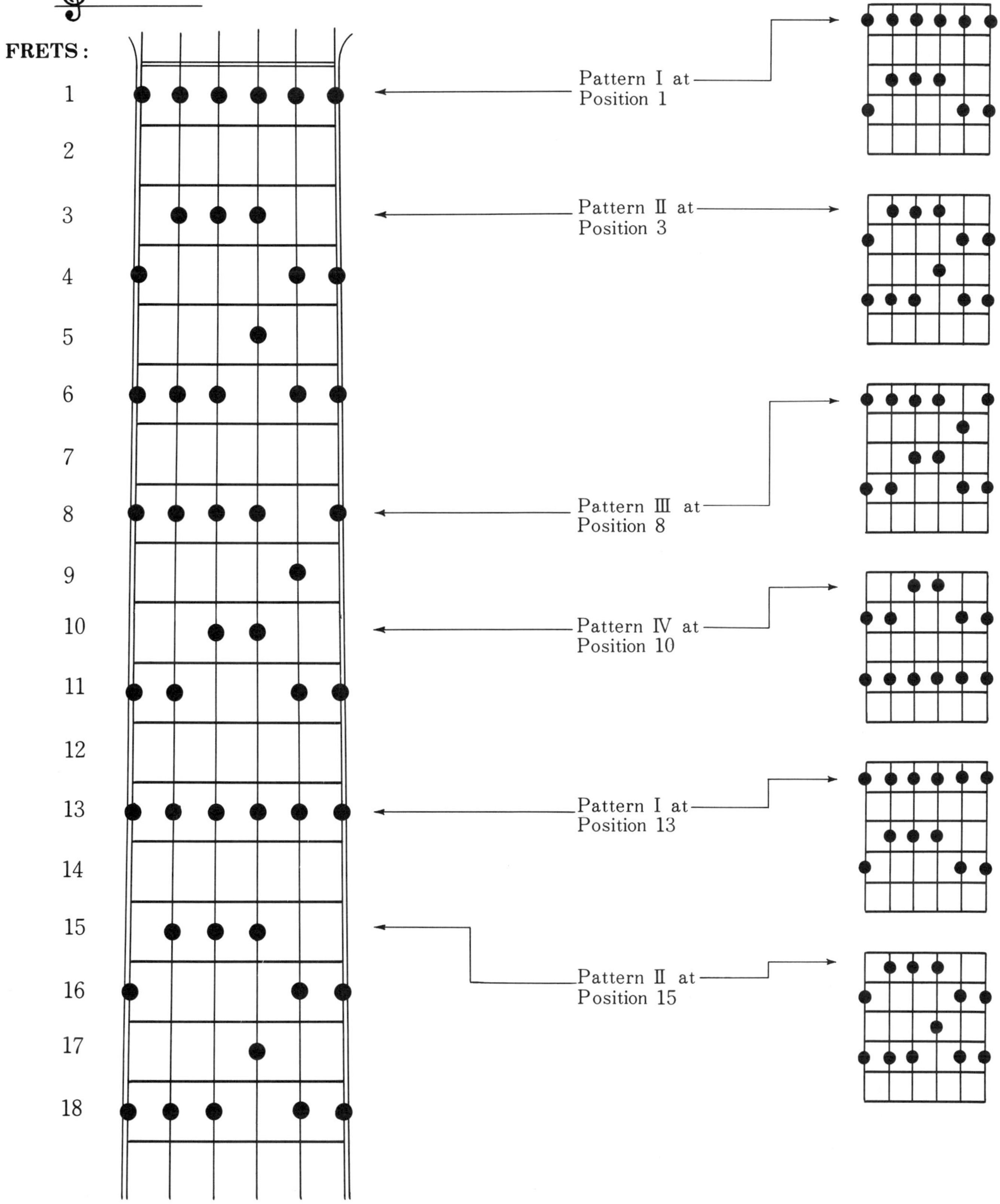

# KEY OF F♯(Gb) Major and F♯ Minor

**Key Signatures;**

F♯  OR G♭ 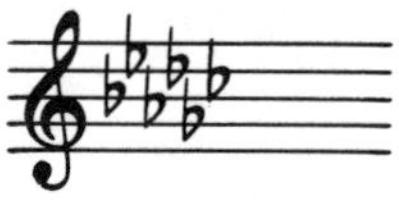

F♯m 

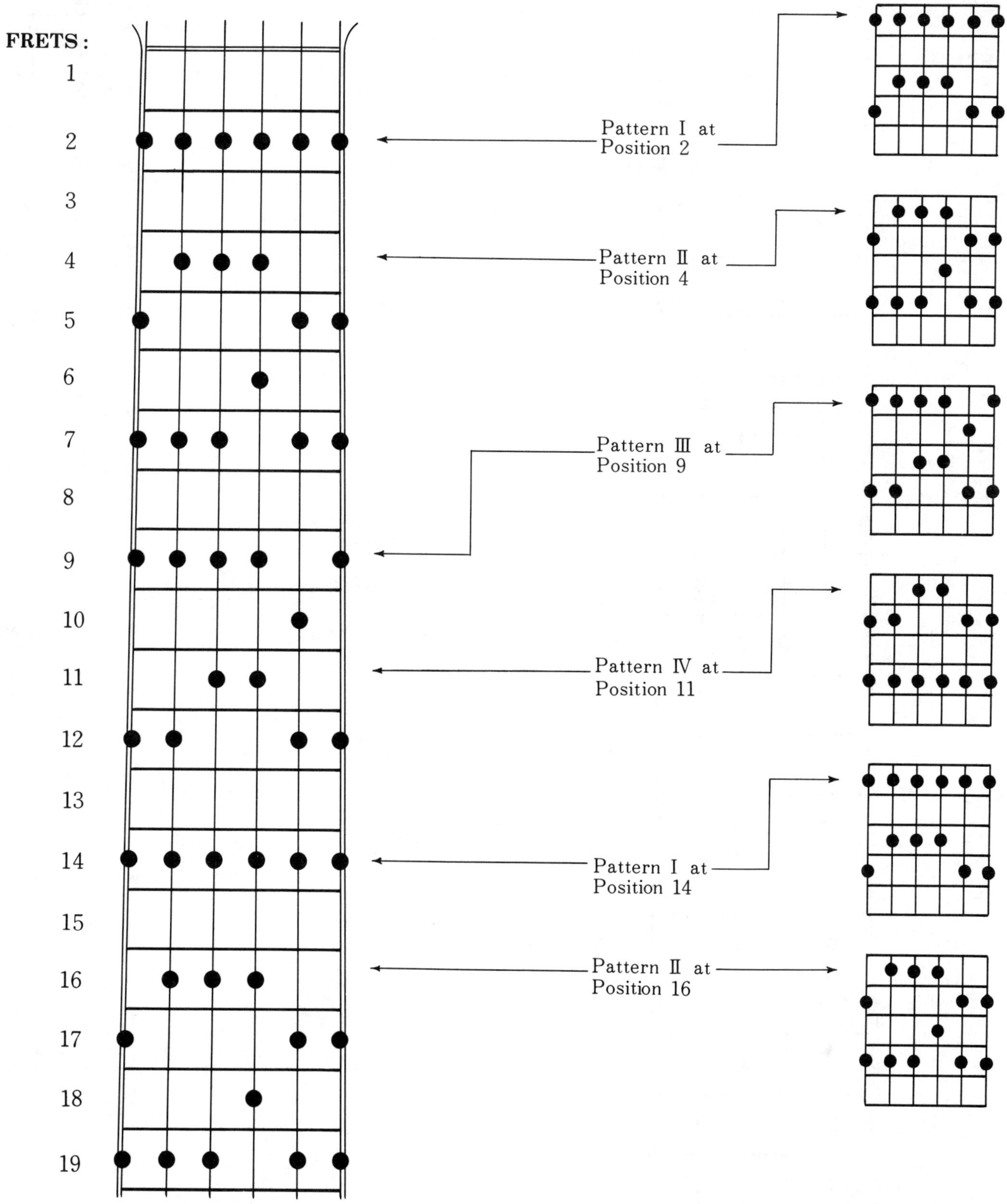

# KEY OF G Major and G Minor

**Key Signatures;**

G

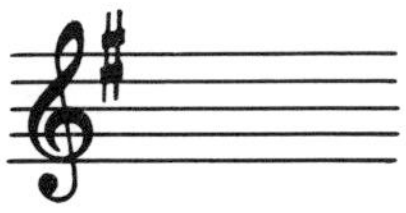

Gm

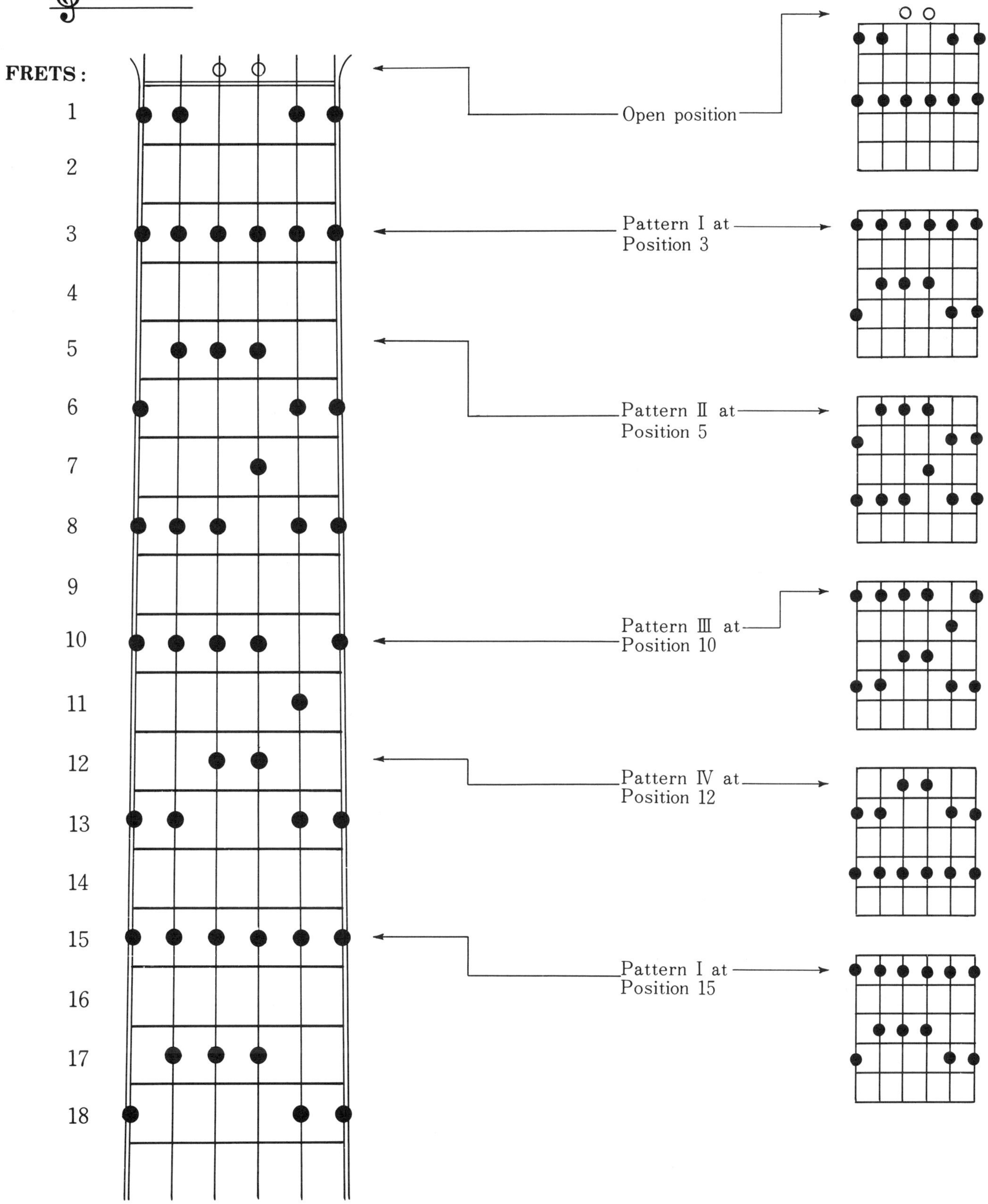

# KEY OF Ab Major and Ab(G♯) Minor

**Key Signatures;**

Ab 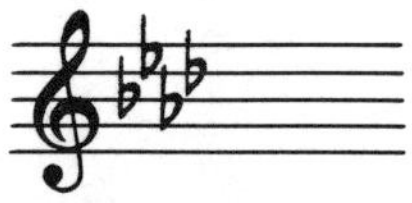

Abm 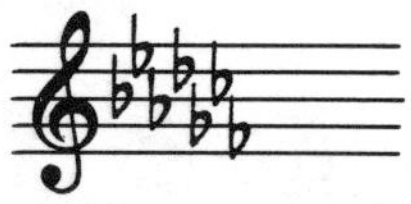 OR G♯m 

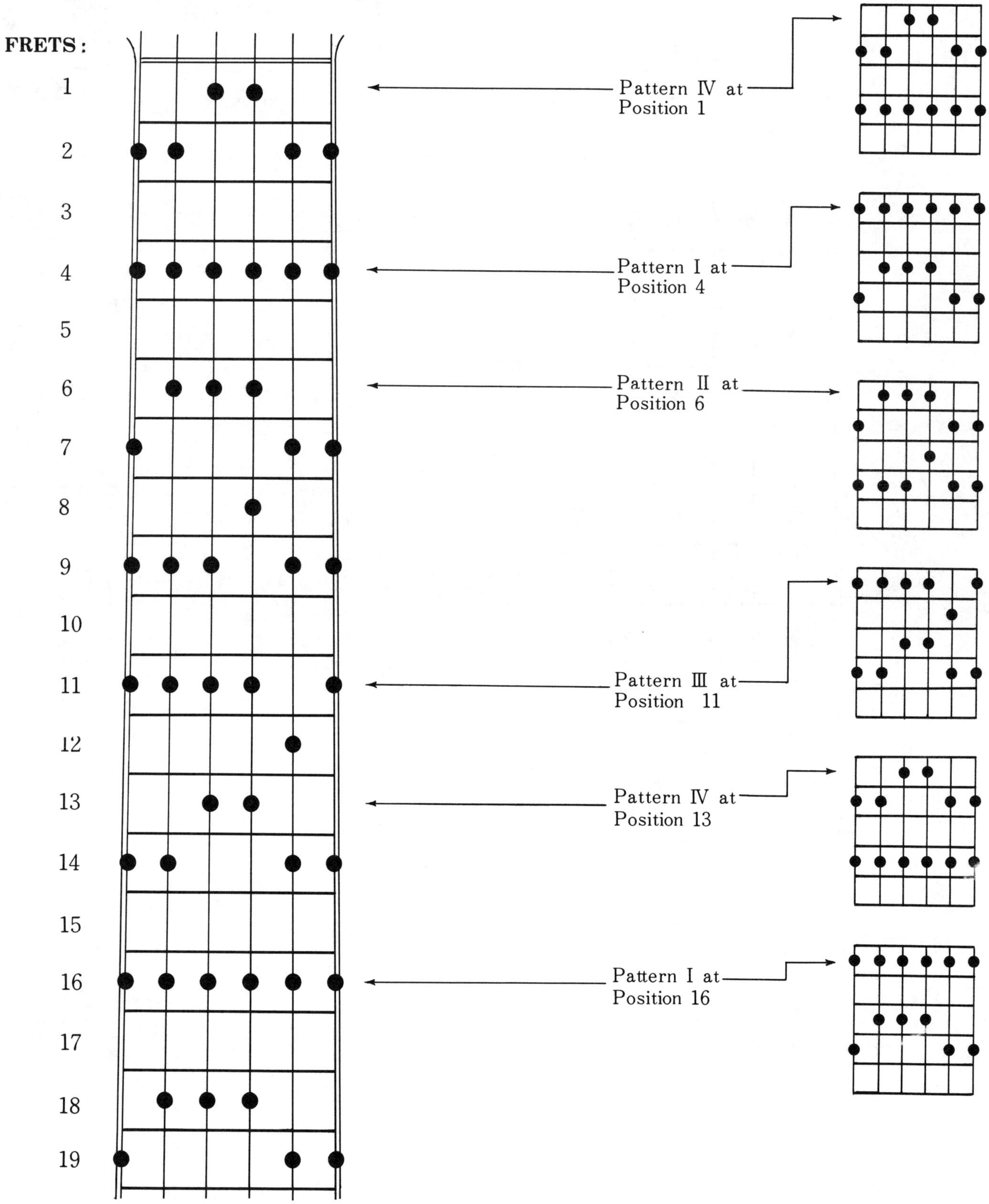

# KEY OF A Major and A Minor

**Key Signatures;**

A 

Am 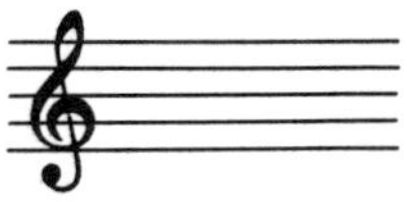

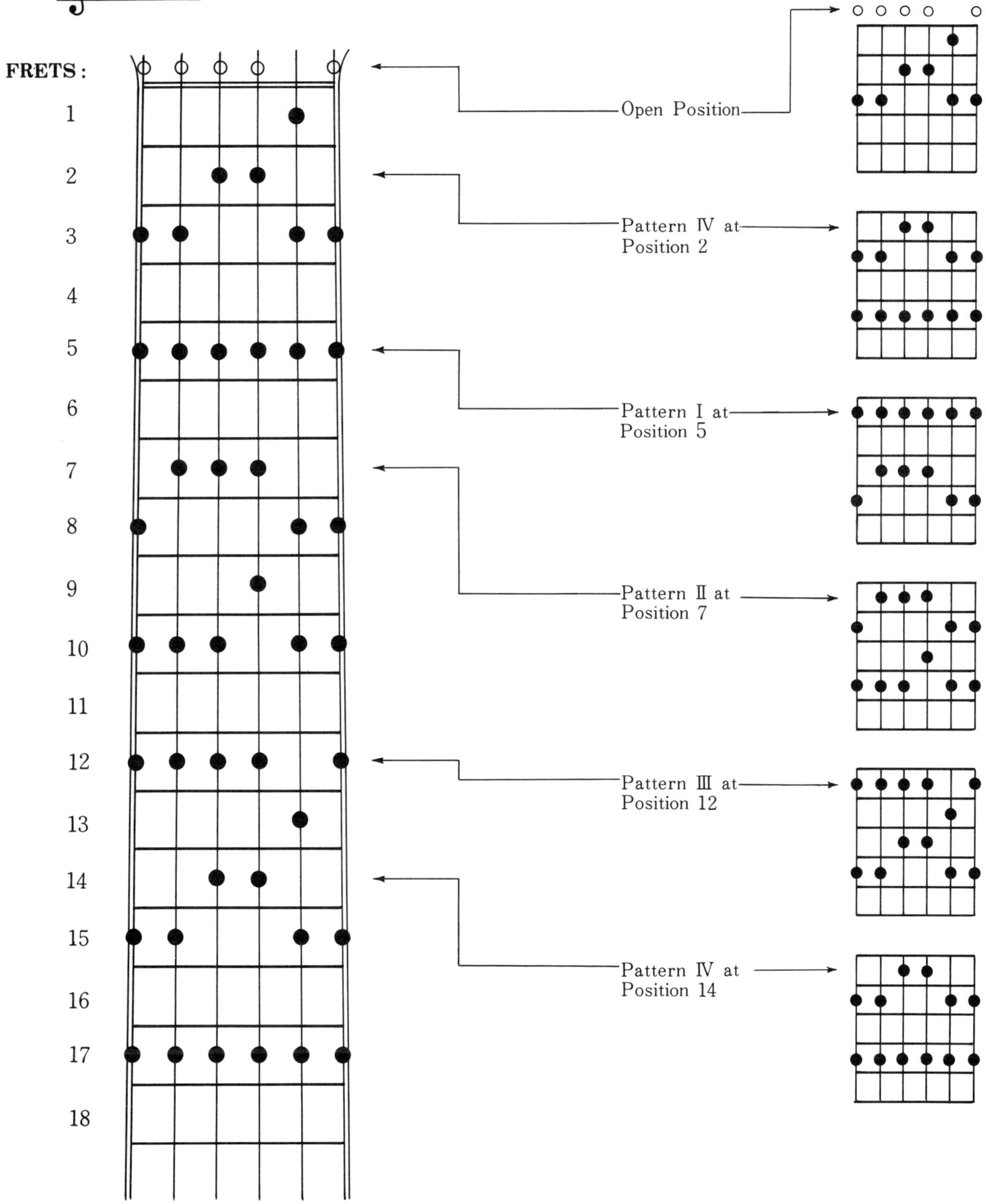

# KEY OF Bb Major and Bb (A#) Minor

**Key Signatures;**

Bb 

Bbm 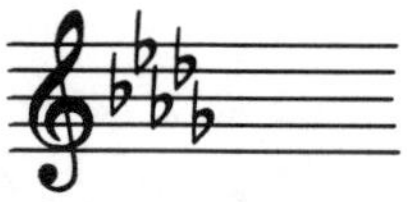 OR A#m 

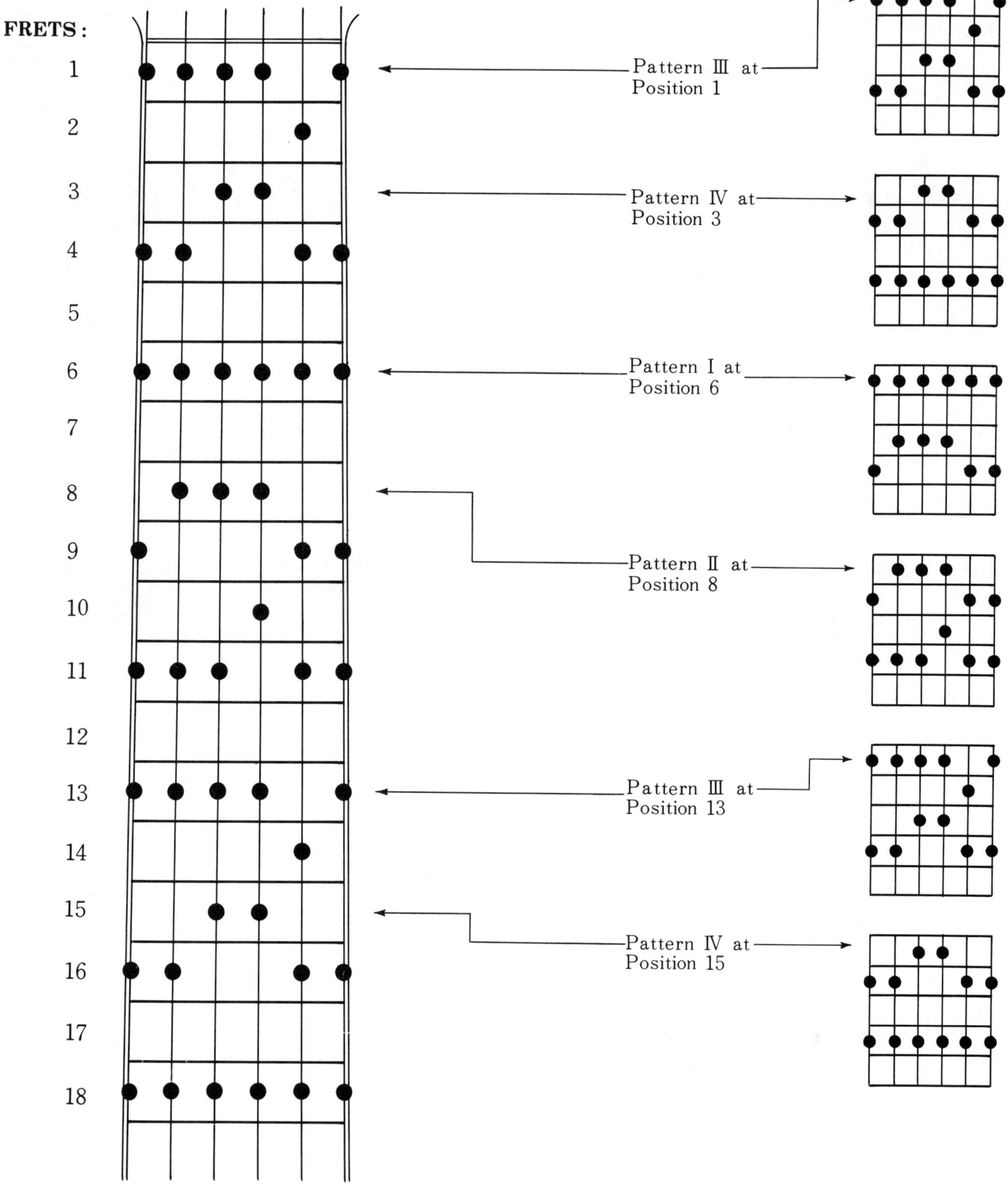

# KEY OF B(Cb) Major and B Minor

Key Signatures;

B  OR Cb 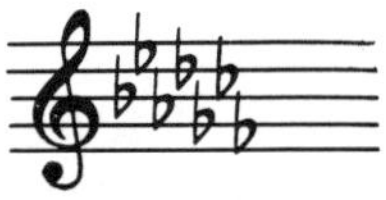

Bm 

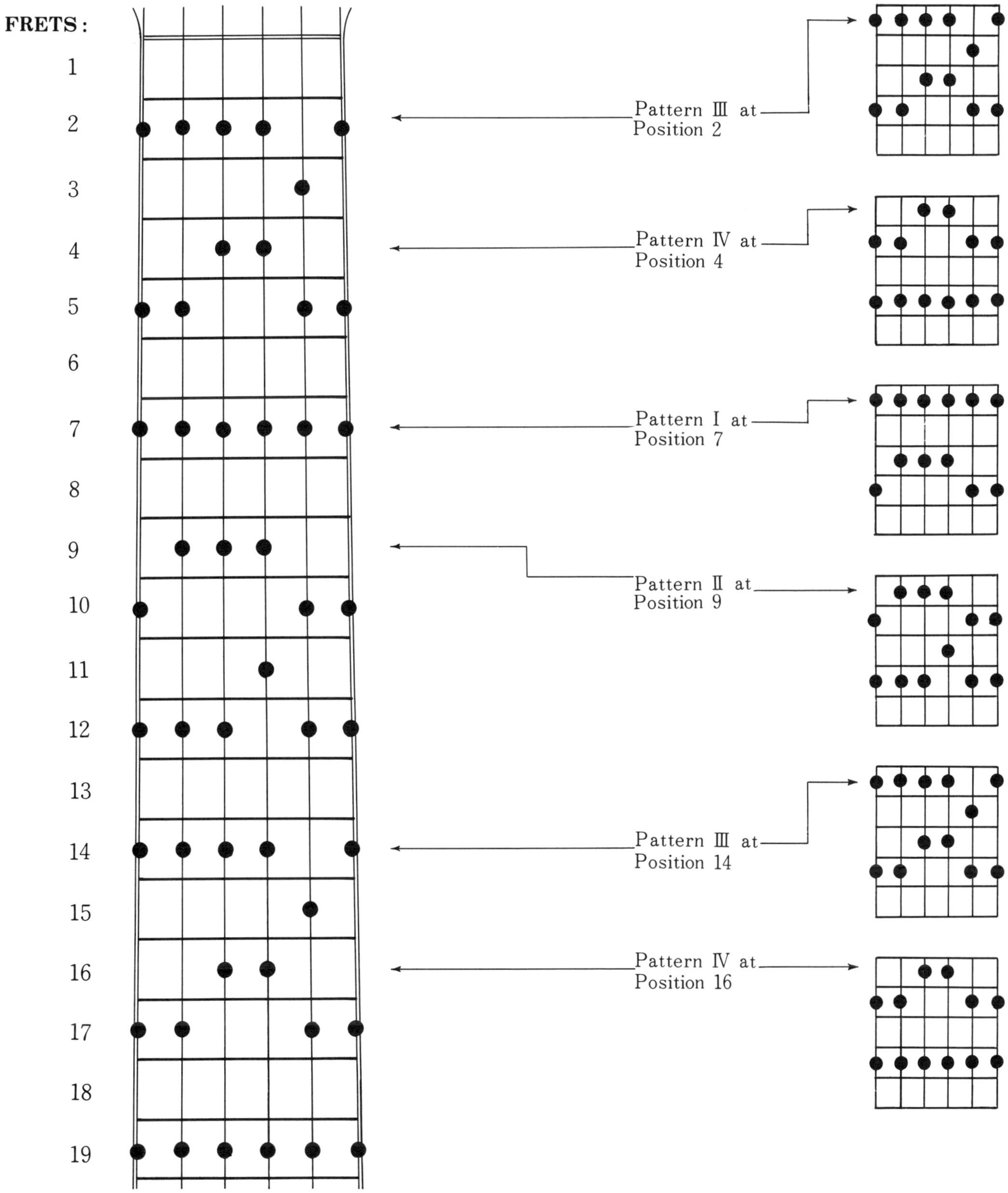

# KEY OF C Major and C Minor

**Key Signatures;**

C

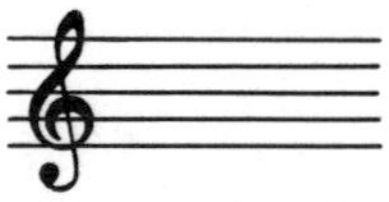

Cm

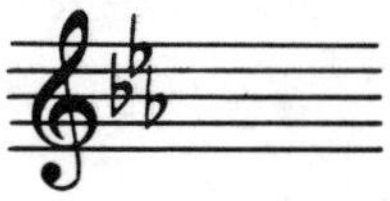

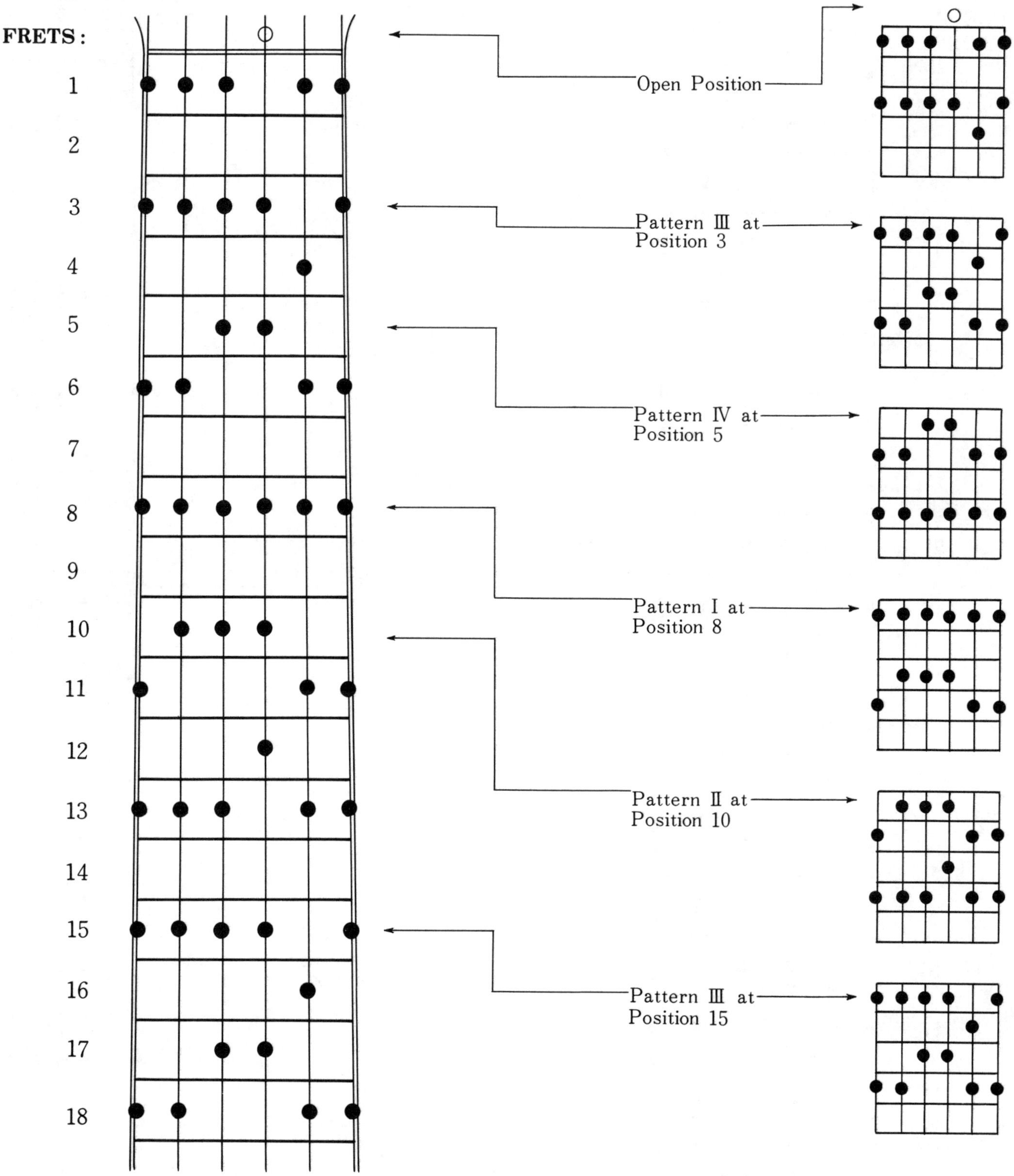

# KEY OF C♯ (Db) Major and C♯ Minor

**Key Signatures;**

C♯  OR Db 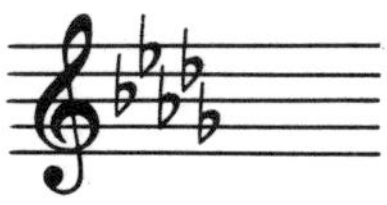

C♯m 

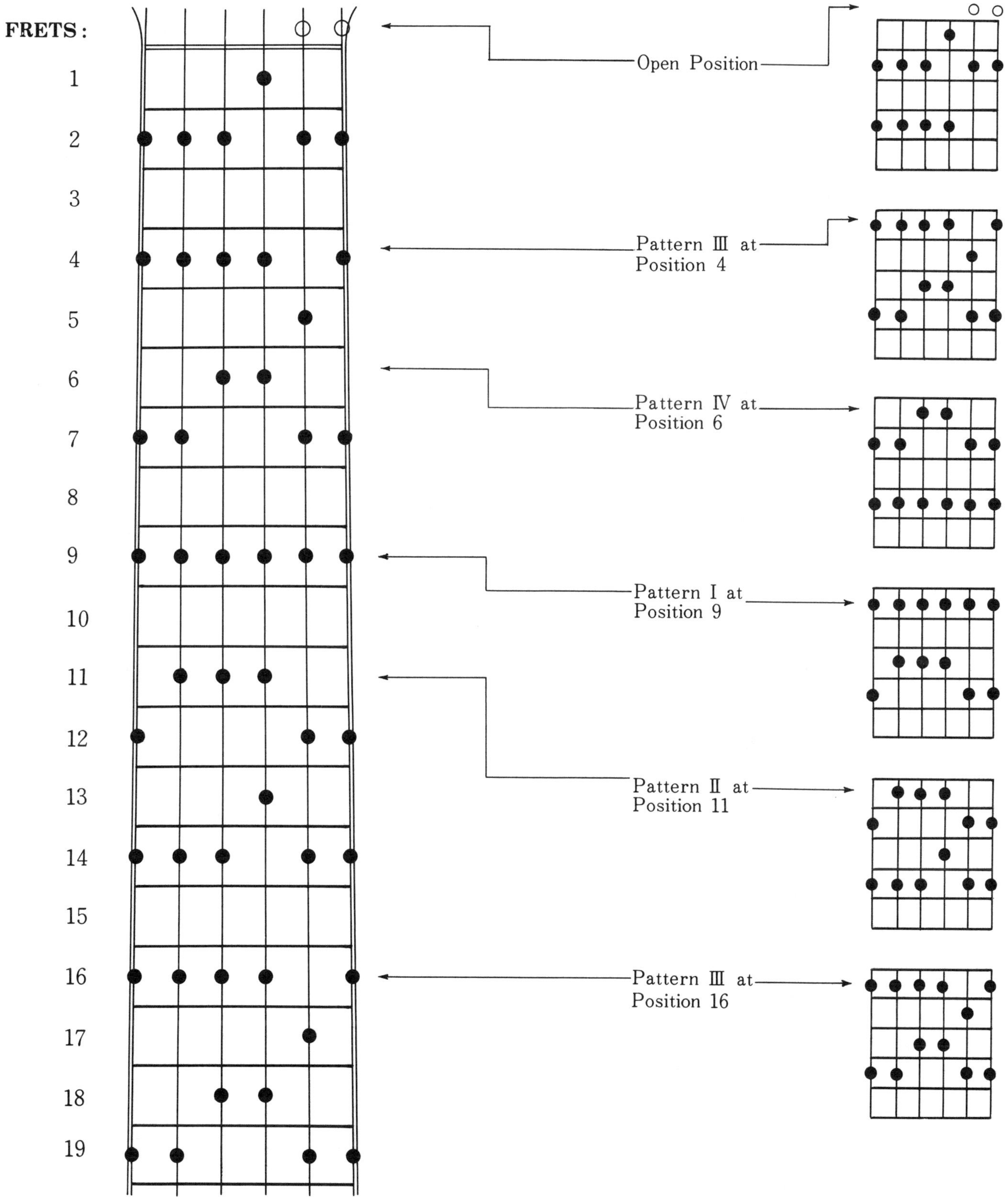

# KEY OF D Major and D Minor

**Key Signatures;**

D

Dm

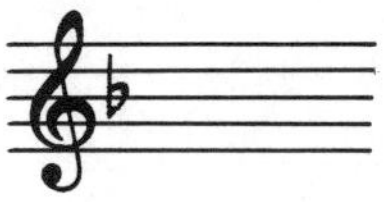

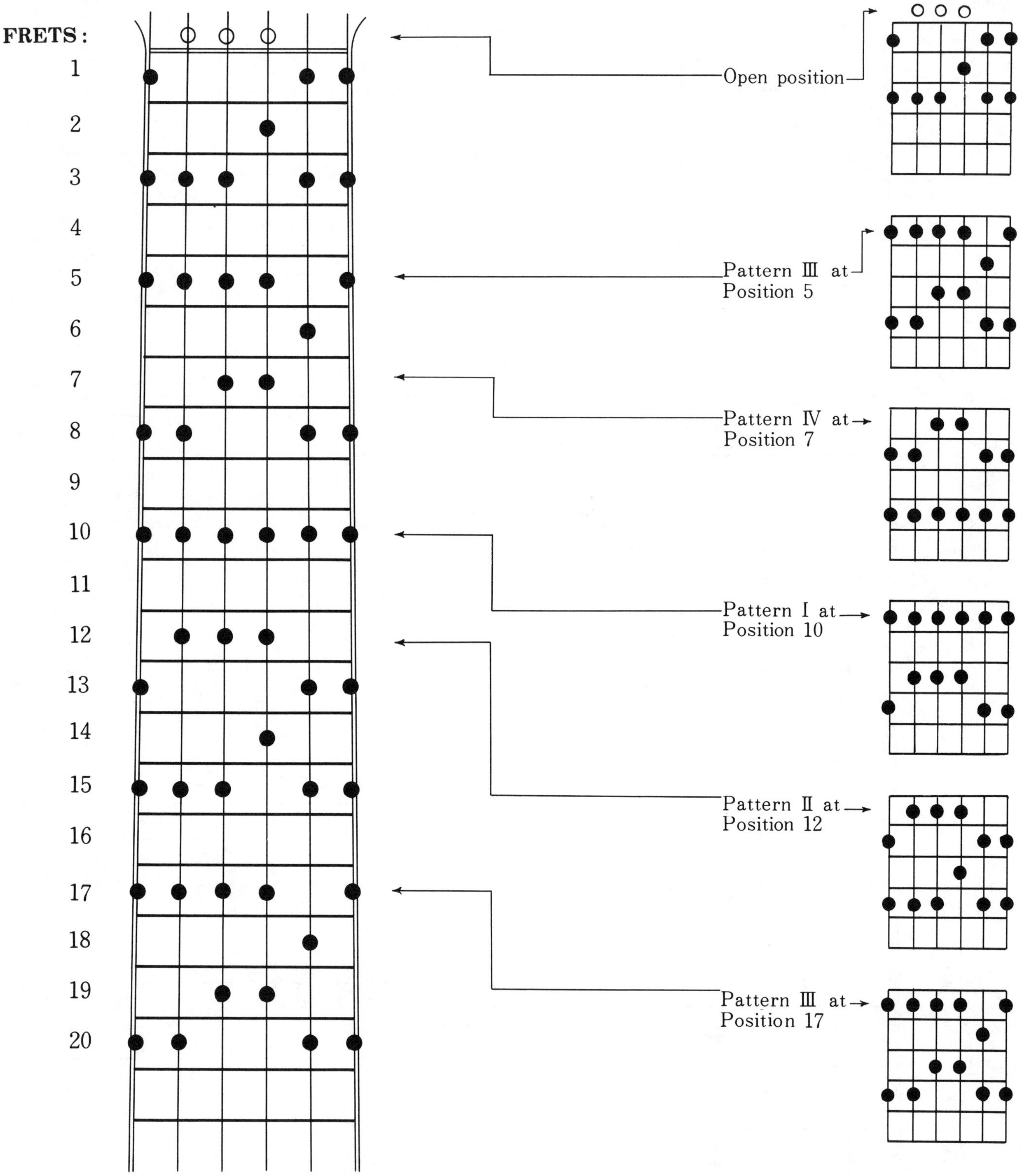

# KEY OF Eb Major and Eb (D♯) Minor

Key Signatures;

Eb 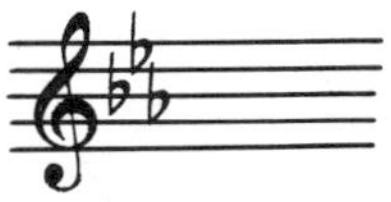

Ebm 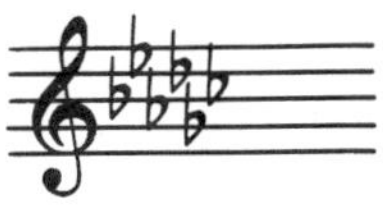 OR D♯m 

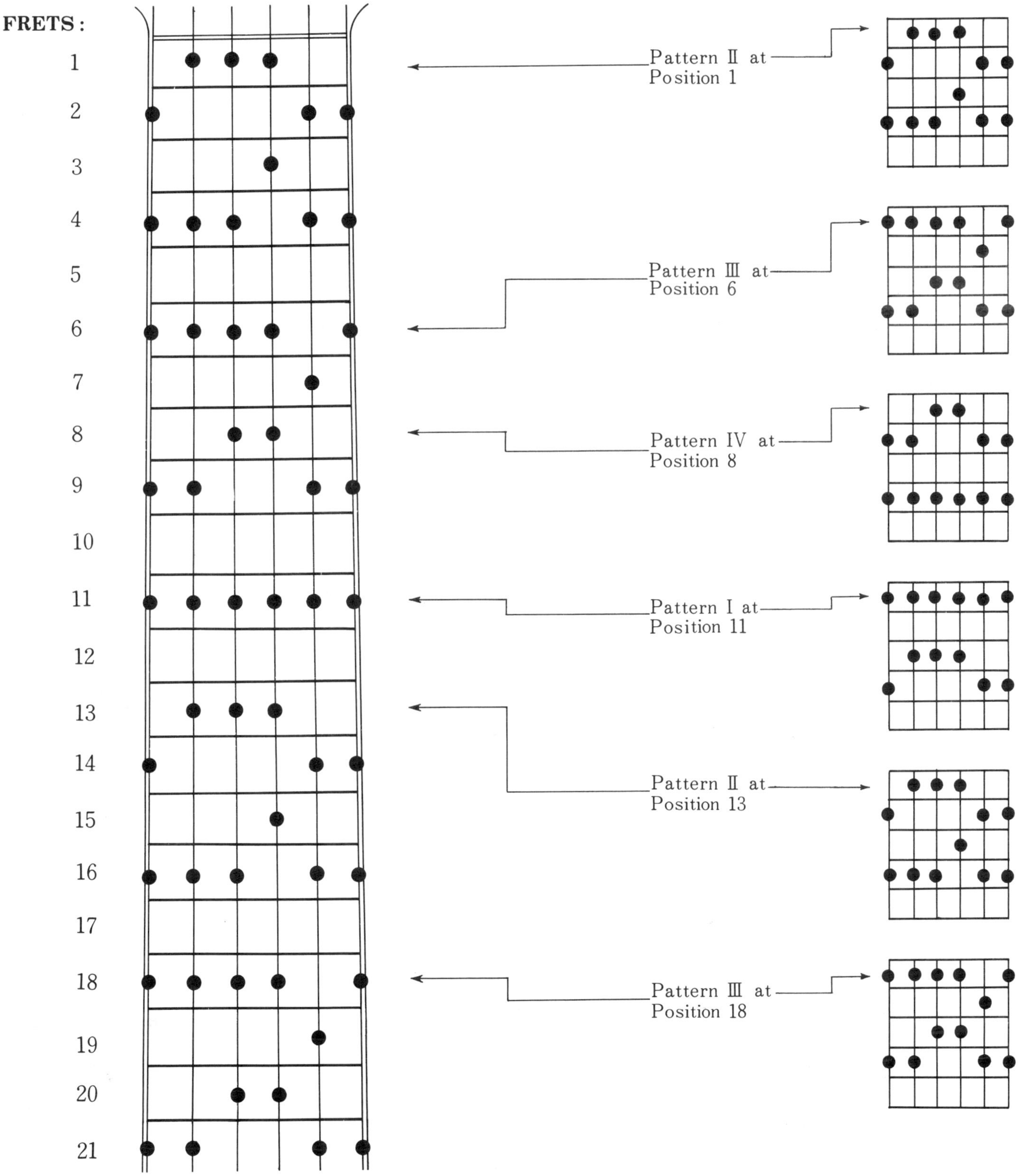

# KEY OF E Major and E Minor

**Key Signatures:**

E

Em

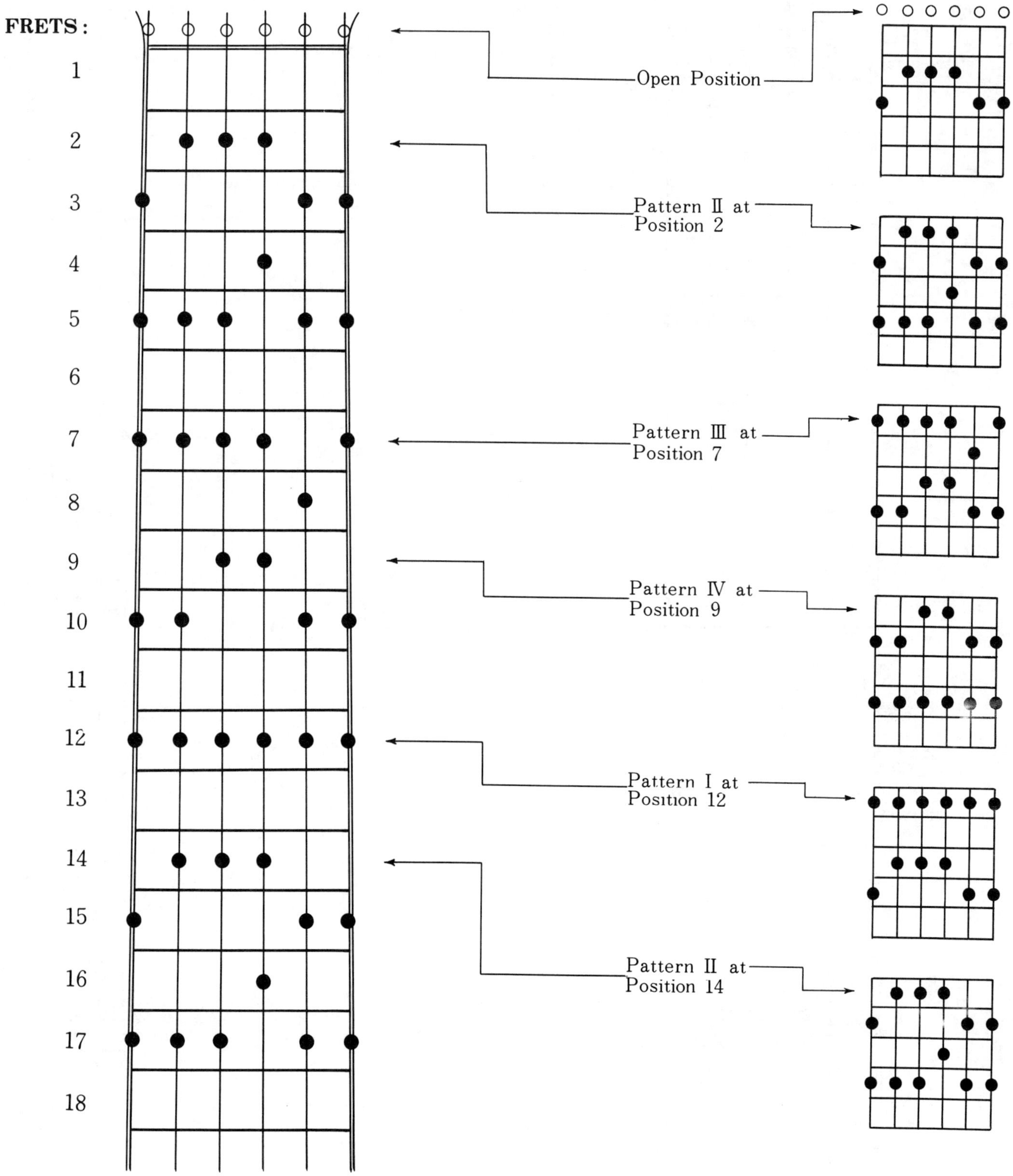

# PLAYING LEAD PATTERNS WITH CHORDS

As a lead guitar player, you must know which Blues – Rock scale patterns to use with the chords of a given song.

Below is a chart that shows the chords for every key that will work with the Blues – Rock scale patterns you have learned.

| Key | | | | | | | | | | | | | |
|---|---|---|---|---|---|---|---|---|---|---|---|---|---|
| F | F | F6 | F7 | Fm | Fm7 | A♭ | B♭ | B♭7 | B♭m | C | C7 | Cm | E♭ |
| F♯ | F♯ | F♯6 | F♯7 | F♯m | F♯m7 | A | B | B7 | Bm | C♯ | C♯7 | C♯m | E |
| G♭ | G♭ | G♭6 | G♭7 | G♭m | G♭m7 | B♭♭ | C♭ | C♭7 | C♭m | D♭ | D♭7 | D♭m | F♭ |
| G | G | G6 | G7 | Gm | Gm7 | B♭ | C | C7 | Cm | D | D7 | Dm | F |
| A♭ | A♭ | A♭6 | A♭7 | A♭m | A♭m7 | C♭ | D♭ | D♭7 | D♭m | E♭ | E♭7 | E♭m | G♭ |
| A | A | A6 | A7 | Am | Am7 | C | D | D7 | Dm | E | E7 | Em | G |
| B♭ | B♭ | B♭6 | B♭7 | B♭m | B♭m7 | D♭ | E♭ | E♭7 | E♭m | F | F7 | Fm | A♭ |
| B | B | B6 | B7 | Bm | Bm7 | D | E | E7 | Em | F♯ | F♯7 | F♯m | A |
| C♭ | C♭ | C♭6 | C♭7 | C♭m | C♭m7 | E♭♭ | F♭ | F♭7 | F♭m | G♭ | G♭7 | G♭m | B♭♭ |
| C | C | C6 | C7 | Cm | Cm7 | E♭ | F | F7 | Fm | G | G7 | Gm | B♭ |
| C♯ | C♯ | C♯6 | C♯7 | C♯m | C♯m7 | E | F♯ | F♯7 | F♯m | G♯ | G♯7 | G♯m | B |
| D♭ | D♭ | D♭6 | D♭7 | D♭m | D♭m7 | F♭ | G♭ | G♭7 | G♭m | A♭ | A♭7 | A♭m | C♭ |
| D | D | D6 | D7 | Dm | Dm7 | F | G | G7 | Gm | A | A7 | Am | C |
| E♭ | E♭ | E♭6 | E♭7 | E♭m | E♭m7 | G♭ | A♭ | A♭7 | A♭m | B♭ | B♭7 | B♭m | D♭ |
| E | E | E6 | E7 | Em | Em7 | G | A | A7 | Am | B | B7 | Bm | D |
| | | | | | | * | | | | | | | * |

* These chords are used only as passing chords for only a few beats in the key shown

To illustrate the above chart, look at some of the following chord progressions in the key of G. As the lead guitar, you can play along with these progressions by using any notes from Blues scale patterns I, II, III, or IV for the Key of G (see reference charts, page 27).

# CHORD PROGRESSIONS IN THE KEY OF G MAJOR AND G MINOR

**Progression Number One**

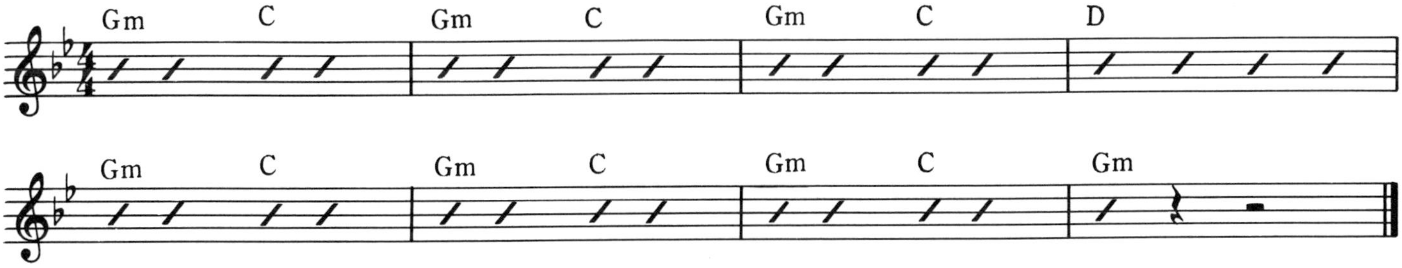

**Progression Number Two**

**Progression Number Three**

**Progression Number Four**

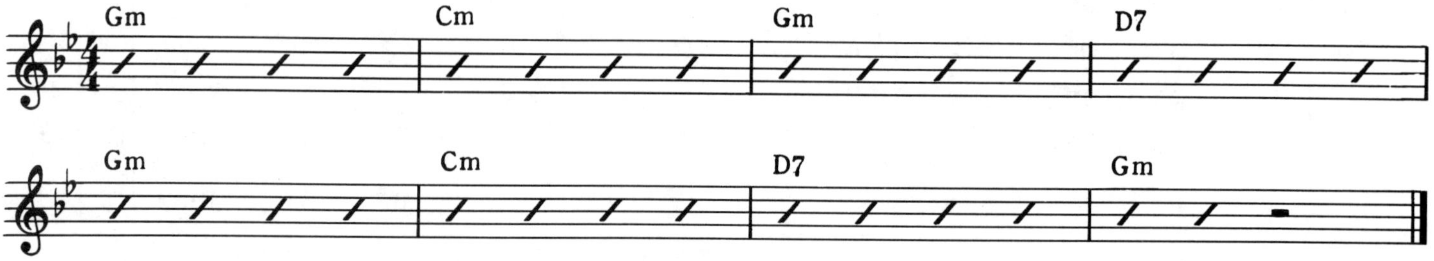


Of course there are many more chord progressions than these shown above; the important thing to realize is that in the key of G, the lead guitar can play G blues scale patterns with any combinations of the chords: G, G6, G7, Gm, Gm7, Bb, C, C7, Cm, D, D7, Dm, or F.

# FOREIGN CHORDS

What happens when foreign chords show up in a progression – chords that are not listed on the chart as working with each key?

Well first of all, let's realize that the scale patterns learned in this book are basically intended for Blues and Rock playing. The scale patterns that have been presented are not intended to work with every type chord and every style of playing that exists – this would be magic.
There are many other types of scales that you may wish to study, for example: major, minor, diminished, augmented, and dorian, to name only a few.

Keeping this in mind, let's see how we can deal with FOREIGN CHORDS when using the BLUES SCALES. The blues scales work with chords that are major, minor, 7th, and m7 in type. Chords that are diminished, augmented, b5, 9th, etc., will not work with the patterns as shown.

| |
|---|
| WHEN A FOREIGN CHORD OCCURS—TEMPORARILY MOVE TO THE SCALE PATTERNS THAT CORRESPOND TO THE FOREIGN CHORD NAME. |

If you are playing in the key of G and a foreign chord such as E7 occurs, then temporarily move to the key of E blues scale patterns for this one chord (see reference charts, page 36).

In the example below, the E7 and A7 are both foreign chords - chords that DO NOT blend with the blues scale patterns for the key of G. Carefully follow how to deal with these two chords.

## KEY OF G EXAMPLE:

CHORDS: G    E7

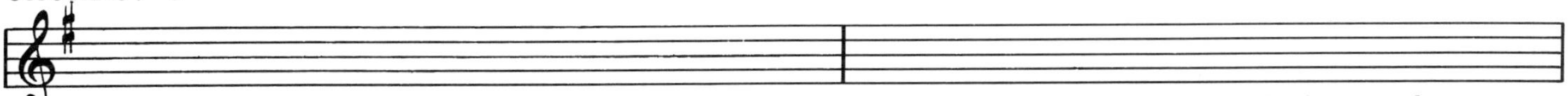

**Lead play G blues scale patterns I, II, III, or IV from the Reference charts page 27.**

**Lead temporarily move to E blues scale patterns, reference chart page 36.**

A7    D7

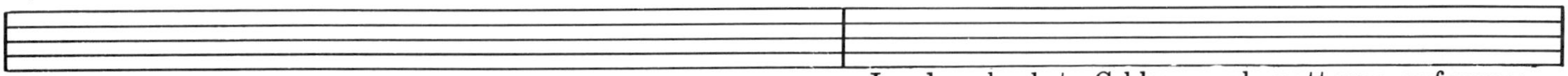

**Lead temporarily move to A blues scale patterns, reference charts page 29.**

**Lead go back to G blues scale patterns, reference charts page 27, because this chord belongs to the key of G. The G patterns blend with this chord it is on the list of workable chords.**

# TWO WAYS TO MOVE INTO A FOREIGN CHORD

When moving into a foreign chord, you may choose to move by (1) "step", or (2) "skip".

## MOVING BY STEP

The example below illustrates the key of G, using pattern 1 at position 3.

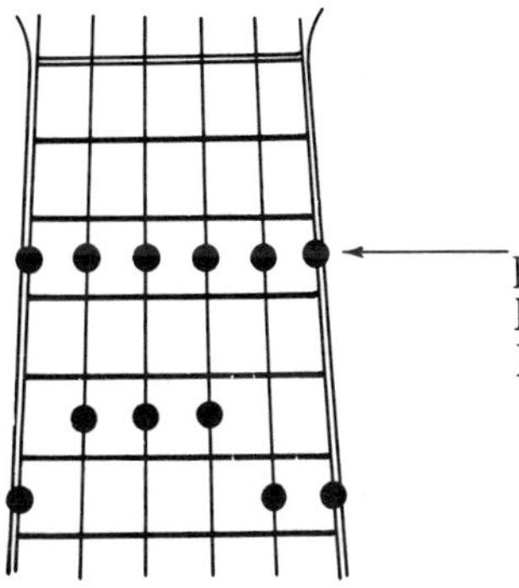

Key of G
Pattern I at
Position 3

When moving, for example, from G to an E7, if you move to the CLOSEST POSITION you would be moving by step. This would be the key of E, Pattern II at position 2.

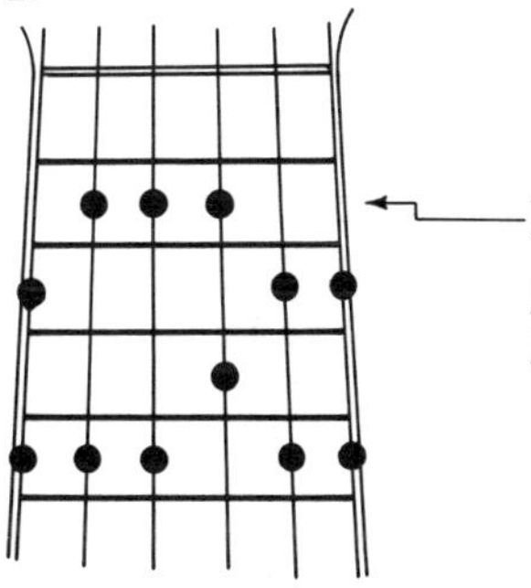

Key of E
Pattern II at
Position 2

# MOVING BY SKIP

The example below again illustrates the key of G, using pattern I at position 3.

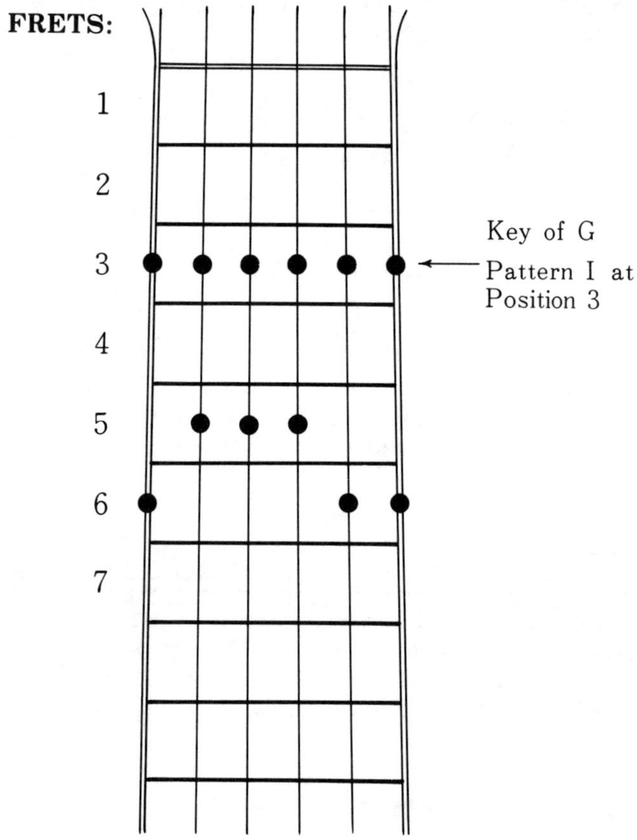


When moving from the key of G to the scale patterns for an E7 by skip, the DISTANCE OF THE MOVE IS LARGE. For example, a skip might be to the 12th position as shown below.

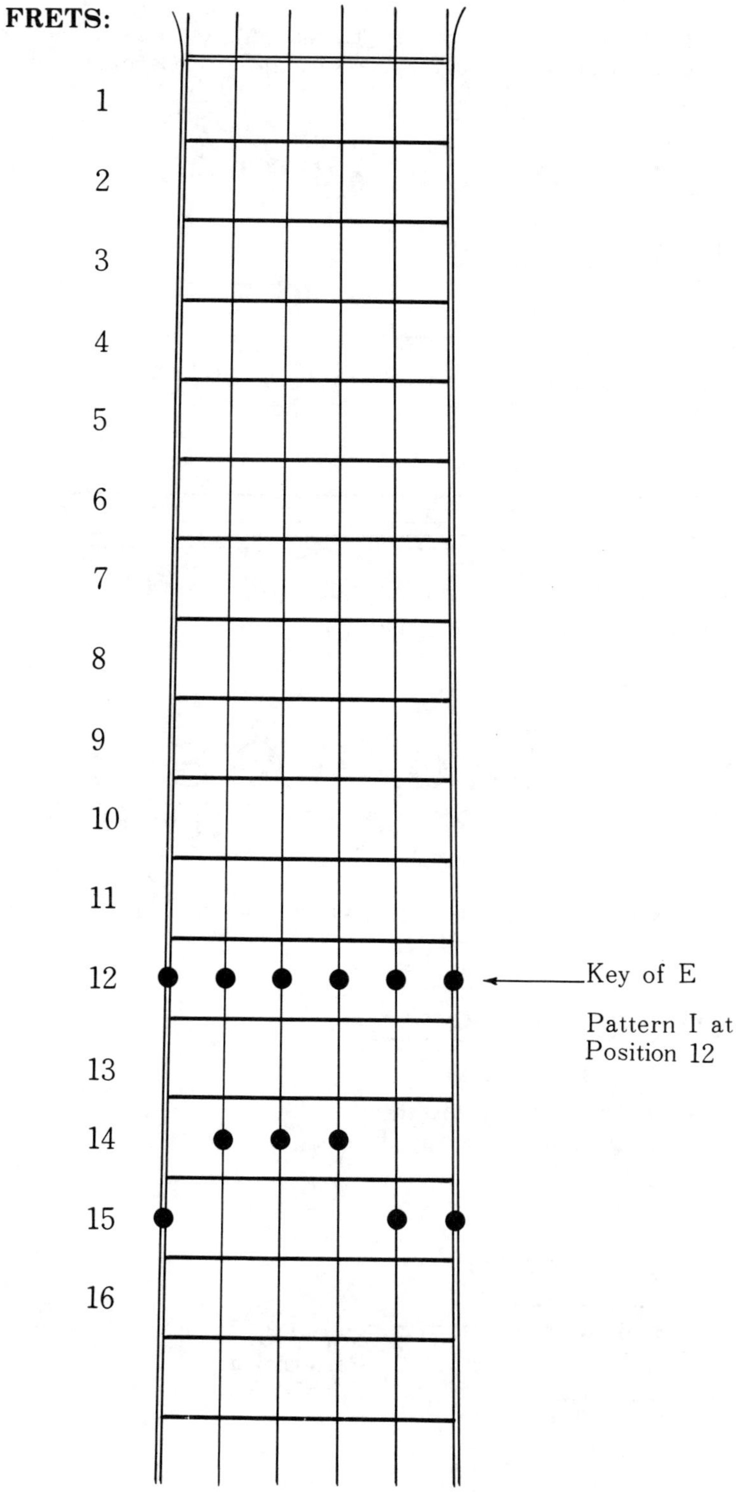

# PASSING TONES

Passing tones are additional notes that you may use when moving from one note to another within the blues scales. Generally, you do not stay on or sustain the passing tones; you move immediately on to the next note. Look at the illustration below:

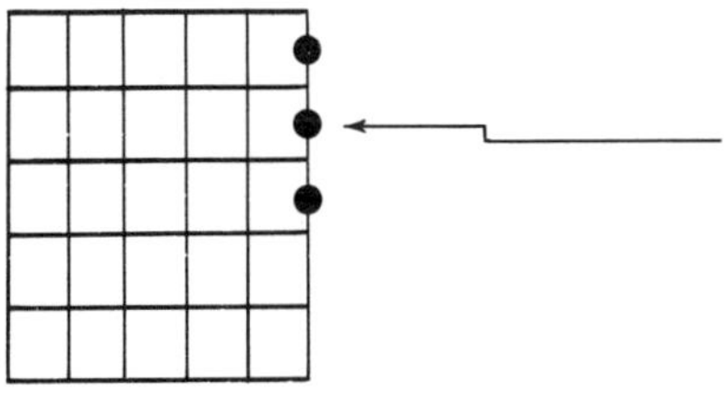

Passing tones may be used between any notes on the guitar that are three frets apart.

Blues Scales I, II, III, and IV are illustrated below with passing tones added. The passing tones are marked by the letter P.

I II III IV

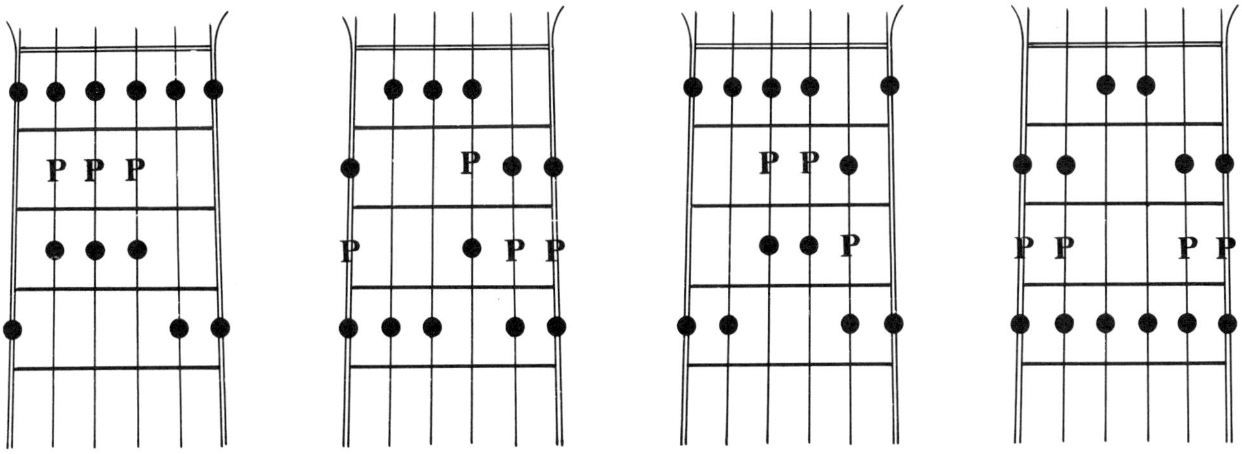

## RECOMMENDED ADDITIONAL BLUES/ROCK STUDY BOOKS

***Blues-Rock Guitar Handbook*** by Mark Lonergan (94172BCD). An excellent introduction to contemporary electric rock and blues guitar, this book lays bare the foundation of modern contemporary rock and blues guitar. Written in notation and tablature. Book/CD Set.

***Rock Guitar Handbook*** by Mark Lonergan (94173BCD). Conveys important contemporary rock concepts with down-to-earth commentary and musical examples. Lonergan explores traditional styles and techniques as well as more recent heavy metal guitar techniques. Written in standard notation and tablature. Book/CD Set.

**Mel Bay Publications, Inc.**
**P.O. Box 66, #4 Industrial Dr.**
**Pacific, MO 63069-0066**